Contents

Introduction

There can be little argument that we live in a consumer society, in which we all utilise a credit facility of one form or another to varying degrees.

We have all grown accustomed to availing ourselves to the use of a credit facility based upon the ' buy now pay later' or 'if you can't afford it finance it' thought pattern. The flexibility it brings is all too welcome and our daily lives financially would be much harder if not impossible without it.

Imagine trying to buy a house without the credit facility of a mortgage: the family car without the facility of hire purchase or the finance agreement; even the smaller class of expenditure via that piece of 'plastic magic' called the credit card for example would pre-dispose us to carrying, on a daily basis, large sums of money around with us. The impracticalities are ten fold.

However, the downside of credit is debt.

We are all to one degree or another in debt but as long as we can service those monthly contractual payments upon the mortgage, credit card or personal loan and the like everything is fine. The problem arises usually through a twist of fate, matrimonial breakdown, loss of job or overtime for example, and we cannot meet those payments. Arrears start building up, accruing interest just exacerbates the situation, creditors grow impatient and before you know it the credit facility has turned into an insurmountable debt mountain.

So what can be done?

What we need to do is look towards ways of getting out of debt. Easier said than done is usually the answer. That is based upon the fact that the large majority do not know which way to turn or what avenues are available other than change your name, run away and hope never to be found!

Lets look at the workable alternatives.

1

The Consumer Credit Agreement, is it enforceable?

The Consumer Credit Act (the Act), most of which came into force in May of 1985 comprises 12 parts which include, amongst other regulations, the regulating of agreements and their form and content and the courts judicial control regarding enforcement orders in respect of otherwise unenforceable agreement.

The vast majority of personal credit agreements are 'regulated' under the Act, which defines such an agreement as one which is for the sum of £25,000 or less and be between one or more individuals. Which include:

'Budget accounts, bank overdrafts, Credit cards, Hire purchase agreements, Credit sale agreements including those offering interest free credit, Personal loans, Bills of sale, Mail order catalogues, Secured loans, Pawn brokers.'

Under the Act, agreements are required to be in a specific written form and must contain certain terms and notices which make the agreement 'properly executed'. If the agreement is not properly executed as it is referred to they may be unenforceable or alternatively enforceable only by order of the court.

The Act sets down certain formalities, which must be present in any agreement for it to comply with the Act. The following information must be contained:

· a heading which describes the type of agreement
· the name and address of the individual consumer/s and creditor and a signature box
· the cash price of the goods / services

- the amount of deposit paid upon entering the agreement
- the details relating to charges or penalties payable if the agreement falls into default or ends prematurely
- the total amount of credit provided and the interest charge for that credit, along with the rate of interest (variable or fixed)
- the annual percentage rate (APR)
- the repayment details relating to the agreement
- the situation regarding cancellation rights of the consumer
- the situation if the agreement is paid off earlier than agreed
- the details of any security provided upon entering the agreement

If, for example, these items are not included then the agreement referred to is an 'improperly executed' agreement and could be totally unenforceable.

Therefore a regulated agreement is referred to as a 'properly executed' agreement if it complies with all the formalities of the Act. However if the required formalities under the Act are not complied with the agreement in question is known as an 'unexecuted' or 'improperly executed' agreement. Any improperly executed agreement can either be totally unenforceable or can only be enforced through an order of the court.

Due to the fact that numerous credit facilities exist which fall under the provisions of the Act the exact content of the prescribed information which should be contained within the body of the agreement can differ and certain agreements are exempt from adhering to some of the formalities as laid down under the Act which include:

- the arrangement with the bank regarding an overdraft facility
- a non-commercial arrangement. This is an agreement made by a creditor / employer who is not in the business of providing credit facilities as part of the business she/he operates and includes any business. For example an employer who regularly makes loans to her/his employee will fall under this category.

· those agreements which are deemed to be 'small agreements' under the Act. These would be where the total credit facility provided, excluding interest and other charges, do not exceed £50.

One of the fundamental formalities of any regulated agreement is that the agreement must be signed by both the lender and the individual consumer. If however the agreement is not signed then it is totally unenforceable. A faulty agreement may sometimes be enforceable, but an unsigned or unwritten agreement is never enforceable.

With regards to signatures there must be a box for the customers signature and where more than one individual is party to the agreement, all are to sign. The lender normally signs outside the box, but not always. The box in question must specify what type of credit agreement the consumer is signing and display a warning that they will be signing a legally binding agreement. The wording within the box would be for example:

> *This is a credit agreement regulated by the Consumer Credit Act 1974.*
> *Sign only if you want to be legally bound by its terms.*
>
> *Signature(s) of Purchaser(s)*
> *Date(s) of Signature(s)*

Signing the agreement itself.

When an agreement is presented to the individual to sign the following rules apply under the Act.

· If the agreement given to the individual by the creditor to be signed is signed there and then but is not signed by the creditor at that point, then a copy of the agreement must be given to the individual, at which point the agreement is unexecuted. A copy of the properly executed agreement must be sent to the individual within seven days of the date of the creditors signature being placed on the agreement. The agreement then becomes executed at this point of the creditor signing.

- If the agreement is sent to the individual to sign and the creditor has not signed, then once the individual has signed a copy of the agreement containing the creditors signature must be sent to the individual within seven days of the creditor signing the agreement. The agreement becomes executed at the point when the creditor signs.

- If the agreement is signed by both the individual and the creditor at the same time a copy of the fully executed agreement must be given to the individual at this point and no further copy needs to be sent to the individual. The agreement becomes binding at the point of both parties signing.

- If the individual is sent the agreement which contains the creditors signature and requires the individuals signature the agreement becomes fully executed at the point of the individual signing the agreement and no further copy is required to be sent.

It should no doubt have become apparent that even with this very basic overview of the Act, there are an abundance of formalities that must be complied with for any agreement to be 'properly executed'.

Therefore with any regulated agreement there is always the possibility of reducing liability or denying all liability. If it is felt that there is any discrepancy over a consumer credit agreement then it is advised that professional advice be sought.

Getting out of an agreement

The ability of a person who has entered into a consumer credit agreement (i.e. just signed the agreement) to cancel that agreement will depend upon certain factors such as: where and when the agreement was signed along with, whether both the trader/retailer and the individual signed at the same time.

The following will give some idea of a situation the individual may be presented with:

A) The individual who signs the agreement at the traders business premises and the trader signs at the same time means that both are bound by the agreement and no cancellation right exists.

B) The individual who signs the agreement at the traders premise but the trader does not sign, usually because the trader will want to do a credit check before committing to the agreement. In this situation it is vital to contact the trader as soon as possible to inform him or her of the withdrawal. Failing to inform the trader of the withdrawal from the agreement prior to the traders signing will mean that the individual is bound by the agreement.

C) If the individual signs the agreement in their home or anywhere other than the traders premises there is a right to cancellation. The cancellation right, commonly referred to as the 'cooling off' period gives the individual the right to cancel the agreement within a set period of time.

The 'cooling off' period lasts for a period of five days. The five day period does not start to run until the individual has received a second copy of the agreement. The first copy of the agreement will have been given to the individual at the time of signing which must include a notice relating to cancellation rights.

The second copy of the agreement, as above mentioned, must be delivered to the in individual by post. The five day period does not include the day the second copy was received, but starts from the following day.

D) If the individual has entered into any agreement, which was made because of an 'unsolicited' visit (i.e. the individual did not request the trader/sales representative to call). Any agreement entered into in these circumstances will have a seven day 'cooling off' period.

If the visit to the individuals premises by the trader was due to an unrequested telephone call made by the trader then this will be classified as an 'unsolicited visit' (i.e. you received the unsolicited telephone call in the first place which led to the visit).

A visit by a trader to an individuals premises will also be classified as 'unsolicited' if for example the trader came to your home at your invitation to conclude an agreement over a new bathroom suite yet leaves with an agreement for a different purpose such as a fitted kitchen.

The agreements covered by the above are the majority of cash or credit agreements over the sum of £35 and up to and including £15000. They do not for example cover any agreement for and relating to the sale of food, drink and other items which can and are supplied via regular rounds. Other situations which do not fall under the above include loans related to and for the purchase of land, insurance contracts; investment agreements under the Financial Services Act 1986; Catalogues or contracts related to building works (double glazing is not classified as building works).

To cancel the agreement the individual must give notice in writing to the credit company directly or to their agent such as the sales person who negotiated the agreement. The cancellation takes effect from the moment the notice is posted and not at the time it is received by the trader or credit company. This, if done within the 'cooling off' period, will bring the whole agreement to a close and no liability remains with the individual.

Any deposits paid by the individual must be returned in full upon receipt of the notice of cancellation.

To be safe it is wise to use some form of registered or recorded postage as proof that the notice of cancellation was dispatched.

Harassment by creditors
It is not uncommon for creditors, debt collection agencies, bailiffs and

solicitors to harass debtors in the pursuit of recovering a debt. There is however a fine grey line between harassment and legitimately pursuing the debtor for the money owed.

The Protection From Harassment Act 1997 states;

'A person must not pursue a course of conduct which amounts to harassment of another and which he knows or ought to know that it amounts to harassment of the other'.

This is further clarified in the Act which states, for the purposes of the above;

' The person whose course of conduct is in question ought to know that it amounts to harassment of another if a reasonable person in possession of the same information would think the course of conduct amounted to harassment of the other'.

The 'course of conduct' referred to above is defined, under the Act, as conduct on at least two occasions and includes speech.

Harassment would include: alarming or causing the person distress which would incorporate persistent abusive telephone calls, verbal abuse in a public place, uninvited visits to the persons house.

Although it would appear, at face value, the Act would or could provide an avenue of address for the aggrieved debtor it is largely watered down by the fact that contacting debtors regarding the debt would ordinarily be deemed a reasonable course of action by the creditor or agents.

It may however be possible to use the act if for example the creditor makes attempts to gain payment from the debtor where an excessive number of demands have been made in a very short period of time. However until the Act has been used and the courts have ruled upon certain issues related to the collection of debts it remains unrealistic to creditor or agents.

It may however be possible to use the act if for example the creditor makes attempts to gain payment from the debtor where an excessive number of demands have been made in a very short period of time. However until the Act has been used and the courts have ruled upon certain issues related to the collection of debts it remains unrealistic to attach any real strength to the Act when challenging the collection techniques used by the creditor and / or agent in respect of outstanding debts.

This leads to reliance upon the existing avenue which falls under the Administration of Justice Act 1970, which defines harassment as:

" attempting to coerce a person to pay a debt by making demands for payment which are calculated to subject the person to alarm, distress, or humiliation due to the frequency, publicity or manner' in which they are used".

Harassment can occur where the creditor or one of its agents make repeated telephone calls or personal visits during unsociable hours, making calls to neighbours or places of the debtors employment along with divulging information regarding the debt to neighbours and employers.

If it is felt that the individual is being harassed the creditor should be contacted immediately pointing out the nature of the complaint and request it be rectified. If the notification has no effect the individual should contact the Trading Standards with the complaint.

Other avenues, which could be pursued with regards to harassment, are contacting the trade association directly.

Credit Services Association
This is a trade association, which governs, by a code of practice, the

Apart from what the CSA does for its members it also has a disciplinary procedure should any complaints be made by the consumer you. The procedure sets out things like how members should behave towards its clients, you, along with how collections should be carried out which include the following;

* Not use oppressive or intrusive collection procedures.
* Be circumspect (cautious) and discreet when attempting to contact the debtor whether by telephone or by personal visits.
* Not act in a manner in public intended to embarrass the debtor.
Unless instructed otherwise accept all reasonable offers made by the debtor to pay by installments.
* Unless otherwise instructed by the debtor not discuss with or disclose to neighbours, relatives or employers the consumer's indebtedness.
* Ensure that all attempted contacts with the debtor are made at reasonable times and at reasonable intervals.
* Not to use improper means to obtain the telephone number or address of the debtor.
* Not falsely imply that criminal proceedings will be brought nor that civil action has been instituted in default of payment
* Not pressurise the debtor to sell property or raise funds by further borrowing
* Ensure that collectors who use pseudonyms (fictitious name) can be identified within the members organisation.

As above stated there is a complaints procedure within the code of practice. The procedure is thus.

The complaint should firstly be addressed to the debt collection company in question. The company must reply, although there is not set time limit stated in the code it should be relatively quickly. If the matter is unresolved the CSA will then take an active roll by directing the consumer to Advice agencies and/or Trading Standards department.

If the complaint is not resolved members of the association can be expelled, should the complaint warrant it. There are few complaints made to the CSA, probably due to the fact that the association and above information is unknown to those outside the debt collection business.

It is possible to get a copy of the CSA code of practice by writing to the CSA: 56 Thorpe Road, Norwich. NR1 1RY.

2
Mortgage and Rent Possession Proceedings.

Probably one of the most frightening experiences that face individuals with rent or mortgage arrears is the arrival of the 'possession summons' and the thought that the home is going to be lost.

In the vast majority of cases the individual will be aware of the forthcoming summons due to previous correspondence from the landlord or mortgage lender regarding the arrears and possible legal action to be taken if the situation is not rectified.

Early negotiations with the landlord or mortgage lender are advised. Upon any notification that rent/mortgage arrears need to be addressed, communication should start. At this point in time the landlord or mortgage lender will, usually, be agreeable to receive the monthly/weekly contractual payment plus an additional sum towards the arrears.

However if the 'ostrich' approach is taken such as burying ones head in the sand and hoping it will all go away, be prepared for the arrival of the 'possession summons'.

The 'possession summons' itself will state a time and date for the court hearing which will be accompanied by a 'particulars of claim' which will contain detailed information relating to:

Mortgages:

A) The date the mortgage was taken out and the property in question.

B) Whether or not the loan falls under the Consumer Credit Act 1974 and confirmation that the appropriate notices have been served upon the individual and when.

C) The situation relating to the finances involved, such as the amount loaned on the mortgage along with the amount and frequency at which it is to be repaid.

D) The total amount outstanding upon the mortgage.

E) The rate of interest.

F) The arrears to the date of issuing the summons.

G) Details of the payments that have been missed, along with details of any late payment history if it is one of the grounds to be relied upon for seeking possession.

H) Previous steps that have been taken in an attempt to recover the arrears and or property.

I) A list of any other payments that are required to be made under the mortgage along with any incorporated legal costs and penalty payments.

J) The order the creditor is seeking, which is usually possession of property, payment of the arrears along with a money judgement.

Rent:

A) The date the tenancy was granted along with the property in question plus the contractual rent payable and general details relating to the tenancy agreement.

B) The amount of arrears along with details of amounts and dates regarding non-payment / late payment history.

C) Previous steps that the landlord has taken to recover the arrears and or property.

As can be seen from the above, the particulars of claim contain a lot of detailed information relating to the property and payments. These details should be checked for accuracy.

Accompanying the above will be a reply form for the individual to complete and return to the court. With mortgage arrears the form presently used is an N11M and for rent arrears form/s N11R or N11A if an assured tenant.

Although the reply forms need not be completed, it is advisable to complete and return the form so that the individuals circumstances are brought to the attention of the court. Any additional information not set out in the reply can be brought to the courts attention at the hearing itself.

Completing the mortgage reply:

The reply form is relatively straightforward and goes through a set of questions relating to the particulars of claim along with the individuals personal and financial situation. Although most questions need no clarification certain questions on the form are clarified below as an aid to completion.

Q6 this asks if an agreement has been reached with the creditor.
If any agreement has been reached and any payments to this effect have been made it is worth attaching a letter to the reply requesting the court adjourn the hearing. It is helpful if the creditor could also be convinced to request an adjournment.

Q8 this question asks if a request for installment payments is made.
This should always be asked for.

Q9 this asks the individual to state the amount, in addition to the contractual payments that is offered towards the arrears.

If an additional amount can be offered it should be stated here. If however, due to the financial circumstances, there is no available income to make an offer towards the arrears an attached letter to the reply form should be made stating either:
* a request to suspend the order for possession on the payment of £X towards the arrears each month and the date of the first payment.

* a request for a suspension of the possession based upon a 'token' payment (i.e. very low offer) towards the arrears for a set period (i.e. the first few months) followed by a more realistic offer after the set time.

Q10 this asks whether the individual wishes the court to consider the agreement on the grounds that the credit facility is extortionate (i.e. exceedingly high interest rate).

Generally this will not be the case even though the individual may feel, in their own mind, it is. If it is felt that this should be requested then further advice should be sought.

Q12-14 these ask for information relating to any state benefits being received by the individual.

Before completing this section it is always wise to check with the benefits agency as to any payments being made and the amount and dates paid.

Q15-26 these requests information about the individuals personal and financial circumstances, other debts and court orders.

Q27 this gives the individual the chance to explain why the arrears arose along with any surrounding circumstances and why it would cause hardship if an eviction from the property was ordered. It is imperative to include anything, which is relevant. For example you would have nowhere to go, lack of other housing in the area, schools; work etc.

Q28 this asks whether the individual would have somewhere else to live if a possession order were to be granted. Always answer this question, NO. That is unless you are one hundred percent certain of permanent alternative accommodation.

Completing the rent reply.
Q1 this asks whether the individual agrees with questions 1 and 2 of the

particulars of claim. The answer should be drafted in the negative as the question states the address of the property but with the rider that the landlord has the right to possession of the property. The answer should be drafted something like:

' I agree with sections one and two in as much as it correctly states the address of my property'.

Q2 this asks whether the individual agrees with the rent arrears as stated.

The arrears should be carefully checked prior to answering this question. The term 'rent' sounds simple enough but note some of the amount claimed by the landlord under this heading may not in fact be so.

Rent can be classed as inclusive or exclusive.
* 'inclusive' would mean that the rent includes other charges such as heat, light and water for example.
* 'exclusive' would mean that the rent is simply payable for the premises.

The tenancy agreement will answer the question regarding the above when checked.

Additionally, if the situation has arisen that over payment of housing benefit has been made. This does not count as rent arrears, but it is not unknown for landlords to include this as rent arrears on the particulars of claim and should always be checked for.

Any rent arrears from a previous property as a result of a property exchange or transfer should again be checked for as these are not rent arrears for the purpose of a claim for possession and should not be included in the particulars of claim by the landlord.

Q4-5 these ask whether any payment/s have been made towards the rent since the issue of the summons. List any payments made.

Q6-7 this is the same as question 6 under the mortgage reply.

Q8 this asks whether a notice seeking possession has been received.
This is formal notification stating that the landlord has the intention to seek possession of the property. The notice must contain:
* the name of the tenant or joint tenants
* the ground/s upon which the possession will be sought (i.e. rent arrears)
* the particulars of the ground/s to be relied upon in sufficient detail so that the tenant can clearly understand the landlords complaint.
* the date at which point possession proceedings will or may begin.
* the name and address of the landlord or agent (i.e. solicitor). This notice should be carefully checked for accuracy.

Q9 this is the same as question 10 above under the mortgage reply.

Q11 this asks if there are any 'counterclaims' the individual has against the landlord. Counter claims may relate to:
* the situation if the rent being paid on a tenancy entered into prior to January 15, 1989 is over and above that set by the fair rents officer. If this is felt to be the case contact with the local authority is advised to establish the 'fair rent' because:
A) the excess amount being charged by the landlord over the fair rent is not counted as rent arrears for the purposes of the possession proceedings, and
B) the amount over and above the fair rent can be re-claimed by the individual for the previous two-year period.
* alternatively any failure of the landlord to honour the statutory obligation to repair the property or other contractual obligation has been neglected. Compensation for these events can be set off against any rent arrears claimed.

If it is felt that either of the above apply it is strongly suggested that further advice is sought.

Q12-15 these relate to information regarding state benefits being received as above under the mortgage reply.

Q16 this is the same as question 28 above under the mortgage reply.

Q17-28 this is the same as questions12-14 above under the mortgage reply.

Q29 this is the same as question 27 above under mortgage reply.

The actual hearing, mortgage and rent.

In respect of the claim for possession based upon arrears the court has to give consideration as to whether, or not, it appears 'reasonable' to grant an order for possession. The court will invariably be satisfied, based upon the documentation before it, that there has been a failure to maintain payment and therefore arrears do in fact exist. The court must still only make an order for possession if given the circumstances, it feels it is reasonable to do so, with the exception of some assured tenancy arrears (see below).

The word 'reasonable' is not defined and leaves large discretion in the courts hands. Factors that will be considered by the court pending the decision will relate to:
* the length of time the arrears have been accruing and how persistent is the failure to pay.
* the personal and financial circumstances of the individual and any previous payment record.
* any agreement reached or proposed regarding repayment of the arrears.

The court will already have the individuals reply form and quite a lot of detailed information relating to the individuals circumstances. However there is no reason why additional information should not be taken to the hearing which may add clarity to the situation as a whole or specific matter.

For example:
* to be armed with copies of a clear financial statement setting out the income and expenditure along with a figure under mortgage / rent showing the actual contractual payment and that figure offered towards the arrears separately.
* Information relating to any improvement into the financial situation expected or hoped for should never be seen as futile such as pending job interviews or applications.
* if any claim that has been recently made in respect of housing benefit or income support mortgage interest which is pending a decision (date of application and any verification is helpful)
* specific family circumstances such as child care.

In addition to the above, the most powerful tool is proof that between the issue of the summons and the hearing contractual payments plus an additional sum towards the rent/mortgage arrears have been made.

After taking all the factors of the case into account the court can decide to order:
A) An absolute possession order - this will state that the individual must give up possession of the property on a particular date, which will usually be set at twenty eight days from the date of the hearing. This can be extended to a fifty six day period if the individual has extenuating circumstances.

Should an absolute possession order be granted the individual should immediately seek advice.

B) A suspended possession order - this will state that the possession of the property is suspended upon terms as set down in the order, which will invariably be that the individual makes payment of the contractual rent/mortgage plus a set additional sum towards the arrears.

C) Adjourn the hearing - this may be done if the court decides it requires further information in respect of the case.

24

D) Dismiss the action - the action could be dismissed if the individuals defence to the rent/mortgage arrears proves successful.

The assured tenancy

The assured tenant falls under a distinct situation when it comes to possession hearings. The following situation described relates solely to assured tenants and those previously protected as shorthold tenants where the tenancy was entered into prior to January 15, 1989.

The Housing Act 1988 sets out mandatory grounds for the possession of property in respect of rent arrears under section 8. It is also possible for the landlord to bring possession proceedings against an individual for rent arrears under section 10 of the discretionary grounds for possession.

If the possession is based upon the discretionary ground (section 10) for rent arrears then the situation as described above will apply.

However if the possession action is brought under section 8 of the mandatory grounds then the following will apply;

The court must make an absolute possession order if at the date of the hearing the individual who pays rent:
* weekly is eight weeks in arrears.
* monthly is two months in arrears.
* quarterly is three months in arrears.

To obtain the obligatory ruling of the court the landlord has to prove;

A) There was the required rent arrears for the stipulated periods (above) both at the time the 'notice seeking possession' was served and at the date of the hearing. If the situation exists then an outright possession order will be granted regardless of the ability of the individual to address the arrears by installments.
The only way to defend the action of a mandatory outright possession order being granted is to, prior to the hearing, reduce the level of

Arrears below that as stated above. This will be the case even if the arrears are reduced by any amount below the limit, even to the extent of £1.00.

Should this be achieved then the court will then be able to consider the situation as described above.

In order to establish the ground upon which the landlord is seeking possession section 3 of the notice seeking possession should be checked.

Equally the tenancy agreement should be checked regarding clauses relating to the tenancy being brought to and end during the fixed term based upon a breach of section 8.

If this is not stipulated within the tenancy agreement then the court jurisdiction is not fettered by the mandatory rule regarding granting possession.

In conclusion. If a possession summons is received make sure it is acted upon as it may take a little time to gather the information required, check the particulars of claim and finally complete the reply form.

Always remember it is not too late to contact the creditor and open negotiations regarding payment towards the arrears.

Even if the creditor states it is to late if the individual can make the contractual payment plus a sum towards the arrears start doing so immediately.

Should it be found that the creditor, especially private landlords, refuses to accept the rent and additional sum make the payments into a separate account of your own, preferably separate from other accounts so it can clearly be seen the payments made and produce this at the hearing.

The above text will have given the reader an insight into the situation of how to deal with a possession summons. However bearing in mind the complexities of certain issues it is always advised that advice is sought at the earliest opportunity.

3

Dealing with the county court summons

If you are unfamiliar with County court Summonses, this brief explanation will aid you.

The summons itself, or properly titled 'Claim Form' is made up of one double sided A4 page with a lilac background. (see pages 38-39) The front page is the actual 'summons' where it will state the name of the company(i.e. creditor referred to as the claimant) and solicitor if addresses differ, your name, (the defendant) the nature of the claim against you, the 'value' of the claim which will be the amount excluding any court costs or solicitors fees, which will be stated as 'I expect to claim not more than £5000", more than £5000 but not more than £15000 or more than £15000 along with the amount of money claimed including any court fees and solicitors costs in the bottom right hand corner of the claim form.

At the top right hand corner will be a number(Claim number) and the name of the court issuing the summons. The reverse side contains a section relating to the 'particulars of claim' which will set out a clear and concise statement of the facts upon which the claimant relies, details of any interest claimed and any other matter relating to the claim being made. The last part of the claim form contains a 'statement of truth' which in simple terms means that what the claimant has set down upon the claim form is believed to be true. A copy of any written agreement referred to must also be attached.

The county court summons (Claim Form) is the most common way in which a creditor will seek to enforce payment of a money debt. The 'claim form' as it is now known when, and if, it arrives will be made up of three forms;

28

The Claim form itself (form N1). This will state the debt claimed along with any further particulars relating to the claim as described above specifically relating to the 'particulars of claim'. These can be served within or attached to the claim form or served separately after the claim form has been served. If the particulars of claim are served with the claim form then the time scales for response as indicated below apply. However if the particulars of claim are not served with the claim form then the following rules and time scales apply;

The particulars of claim must be served by the claimant upon the defendant within fourteen days of the service of the claim form and must be accompanied by the form described below relating to the response pack. The response time (i.e. 14 days) starts to run from the date of service of the particulars of claim, in this situation, and not from the date of service of the actual claim form

The accompanying three forms are headed the 'Response Pack', (N9)', 'Admission' (form N9A) and the 'Defence & Counterclaim (N9B), If the claim is for an unspecified amount or not for money the Admission form will be (N9C) and the defence and counterclaim form (N9D). The appropriate forms will be included within the response pack dependant upon the claim made.

This chapter will concentrate upon those claims made for a 'specified amount' (i.e. the claim is for an established monetary figure).

The Response Pack(N9).
This will give details of what is included in the pack along with what to do and which forms to complete regarding the defendants response. The bottom part of the form will be headed 'Acknowledgement of Service' when and why to complete this form is explained within the 'notes for the defendant on replying to this claim' which will accompany the forms discussed within this chapter.

The Admission form(N9A).

This form needs to be completed by the individual, if the claim is not disputed, and returned to the creditor or their agent (i.e. solicitor if used) as named upon the claim form. Once the form is received by the creditor, which should include an offer of repayment (discussed below), the creditor will either accept or reject the offer made.

If the offer is accepted the creditor will apply to the court to enter judgement for the sum claimed and to be repaid at the installment rate offered by the individual. A copy of the 'County Court' judgement will then be sent to the individual stating the monthly amount to be paid and the date the first payment is due.

If the creditor rejects the offer made the form will be submitted to the court by the creditor and a repayment figure will be set by the court based upon the information entered upon the form by the individual.

This reply form should be sent to the creditor within 14 days of service. The individual (defendant) is deemed to have received the claim form and accompanying documentation on the second day from when it is posted from the court. Effectively the individual has sixteen days from the date the claim form was issued/posted

If the individual does not reply. Once the 14 day period has expired the creditor will request a county court judgement be entered upon his/her own terms, which is usually in the nature of a 'forthwith' payment. In other words the amount of money claimed, including court fees and any solicitors costs, are to be paid immediately.

It is therefore in the individuals best interest to complete and return either the 'Admission or Defence & Counterclaim ' form within the required time limit. With regards to the 'Defence and Counterclaim' response an additional 14 days can be requested by the individual (defendant) if more time is needed to prepare the written defence by completing the 'Acknowledgement of Service' (above mentioned) which is to be returned to the issuing court, which is set out at the head of the form itself. The response on the (N9) is a simple, three choice tick box reply;

1. I intend to defend all of this claim
2. I intend to defend part of this claim
3. I intend to contest jurisdiction

The first two are self explanatory, the third for aid of clarity refers to a dispute over the court to which the claimant has issued the claim form from, for example all claims should be issued from the county court with the exception of; those claims which exceed £15000 and do not relate to an agreement under the Consumer Credit Act 1974. In other words if the claimant issued proceedings via the high court for a claim less than £15000 or any claim connected to a consumer credit agreement would be disputed under 'jurisdiction'.

The actual 'Acknowledgement of Service' (N210) is a double sided A4 sheet which consists of four parts (A-D). The form indicates which part to complete regarding the nature of the individuals dispute.

Initially it will be assumed that the debt is not disputed and the 'Admission' reply form needs to be completed.

The page headed 'Admission' (N9A) contains quite a lot of detailed questions regarding your personal and financial details which are to be completed by you, and at the end of the form at section 12 a space for you to insert an offer of repayment.

The majority of the questions are straightforward and self explanatory, but for aid of clarity they will be looked at noting any specific considerations that should be given prior to completion;

Q1 this asks for the individual to insert their name, address, marital status and age.

Q2 this asks about dependants such as the individuals children and others (i.e. elderly relatives).

Q3 requests details about employment / unemployment.

Q4 this asks for details about bank / building society accounts that are held along with any savings in them.

It is wise to note that if for example wages/salary are paid into an account and are used for living expenses these are not savings. Savings for the want of a better explanation are those funds that do not need to be used. If therefore an account is in credit at the time of completing the reply it is safe to indicate nil funds or at best a couple of pounds. If the account is overdrawn and / or unused then mention this fact.

Any savings which are noted here which are less than;
* one and one half times the individuals monthly income, or
* seven times the individuals weekly income, will, or at least should by the court, be ignored.

Also if the account is in joint names then only those funds belonging to the individual named upon the summons should be noted in this section.

Q5 this asks for the type of property you live in.

All the above questions, as above mentioned, barring question four are straightforward and create little in the way of problems. The remainder of the questions upon the form (6-11) require some serious thought prior to completion.

Q6 this deals with the individuals income, which at face value presents no obvious problems. however the following points should be borne in mind;

* be careful of entering net wages which include overtime or bonuses. These may not last or be at the same rate. If it is the individuals choice to include these additional sums when entering the net sum it is wise to look back over the previous wage slips (i.e. six weeks) and take an average.

* a question that may sometimes arise is, whether or not to enter a spouses or

partners wage/salary as income. If the actual debt is in one name only then, legally, it is the liability of that individual to discharge it. Whether or not to include joint income in this section has to be the choice of the individual/couple involved.

If, only, the net income of the individual named upon the summons is entered then when noting the expenditure (below), only the expenditure met from that income should be listed.

Q7 this asks for the expenditure, on a weekly or monthly basis. The best format is to keep it on the same basis as the income is listed.

When listing the expenditure make sure the figures entered are correct, averaging out certain utility bills such as gas is worth consideration as these bills are likely to be higher in the winter than the summer months.

* To turn annual figures to weekly / monthly, take total figure and divide by 52(weeks) or 12(months).
* To turn quarterly figures into the above multiply by 4 and divide by 52(weeks) or 12(months).
* To turn monthly into weekly multiply figure by 12(months) and divide by 52(weeks), reverse the process for weekly into monthly.

If there is other expenditure which is not specifically listed, then this needs to be listed where it states, 'other expenditure. This however gives a limited space of three lines. If there is not enough space it is best advised to attach a separate income/expenditure statement and writing ' see attached financial statement' through questions 6 and 7 (for financial statements see chapter ?).

As an additional note certain expenditure, if listed, is deemed to be non essential in the creditors and courts eyes. Such expenditure would include for example cigarettes, alcohol, newspapers and children's pocket money. If these or other types of expenditure are made, they should not be itemised separately but incorporated into other headed expenditure. The resultant figure, however, must be seen to be realistic.

Q8 this part of the summons asks for information about any arrears relating to priority debts. This section does not specifically ask for the total amount of arrears, only the repayment rate (per week/month) towards the arrears. If known it needs to be entered here.

If however no repayment schedule has yet been negotiated or agreed, the total amount of the arrears needs to be entered against the priority debt in question.

If this situation arises the court is advised to assume a repayment schedule to clear the debt over a period of months (usually between 3-6 months).

If an arrangement is already in place to pay priority arrears but the actual weekly or monthly figure being taken towards the arrears is unknown because for example the contractual figure plus the arrears is paid as one, then it is simpler to insert the total figure being paid under the expenditure list in question seven and omit any entry in this section.

Q9 This requests the individual to list any court orders. The court claim number and weekly or monthly payment needs to be inserted. If the claim number is not known, rather than leave it blank put 'n/k' in its place. Alternatively it is always possible to contact the issuing court to ascertain the number.

If you are behind in any payments note it in the box provided.

Q10 This refers to credit debts, which include all other non-priority creditors to which the individual is indebted. If there is insufficient space here, simply write 'see attached sheet' and list them clearly stating the name of the creditor, the amount of the debt along with any payment schedule is in place. If there is no payment being made towards the debt simply put 'nil'.

Q11 this asks if you wish to make an offer of repayment towards the sum claimed upon the summons, either in full or via a monthly repayment offer.

If there is some available income (i.e. money left over) after deducting the individuals expenditure from the income, enter the resultant figure.

Note-do not offer more than can be afforded and do not think the offer available is to low. If circumstances dictate the offer of £1.00 per month is not in it's own right unacceptable.

If there is no available income to make any offer, a 'nil' offer can in theory be inserted. If this is done either the court will determine the offer, or if no offer is made the creditor can request the court to enter judgement, by default, on whatever terms the creditor so chooses. It is therefore felt wise to insert a low figure (i.e. £1.00 per month) as above mentioned rather than the court making the calculation.

If the offer is accepted by the creditor the judgement will be entered upon the offer made by the individual. However if the creditor refuses the offer it will be for the court to set the rate of repayment, which may be the same as the offer made by the individual or different given the calculation made by the court upon the information provided by the individual upon the admission form.

Therefore, where ever possible it is wise to insert a figure in the monthly offer box regardless of the monetary size.

Q12 is where the individual signs and dates the completed form.

As a final note, remember that if the admission form is not fully completed and returned to the creditor within the time scale, above, mentioned the creditor can ask the court to issue the judgement, in default (i.e. in other words you have not replied), upon whatever terms the creditor deems fit.

If the inevitable occurs and judgement is entered against the individual upon terms that cannot be met see the chapter referring to county court judgements.

'Defence & Counterclaim' (N9B). There are instructions on the front side of the form on how to fill it in.

It contains 5 separate sections you need to complete;

Section 1 asks you whether you dispute the full amount claimed or dispute part of the claim made on the claim form. You need to 'tick' one or the other.

Section 2 is asking you whether you dispute the claim because you have already paid it, if your answer is 'No' then it tells you to go to the next section, 3.

Section 3 this section/box is referred to below stating the reason/s why you dispute the claim and need to insert the defence to the claim.

Section 4 this asks whether you wish to make a claim against the claimant (creditor).

Section 5 this is for your signature, your address and date.

If the whole of the amount claimed is disputed then only the defence and counterclaim form needs to be completed. If however only part of the amount claimed is disputed ,and the remainder admitted, then both the admission form and defence and counter claim forms should be completed and returned to the court.

Upon receipt of the individuals defence / counter claim form the court will send a an 'Allocation questionnaire' to all parties of the claim. There will be inserted upon the form a date by which the form needs to completed and returned to the court at the top right hand corner. The allocation questionnaire is made up of five pages with an orange background. The first four pages ask a series of questions (A-J), the fifth page holds the notes upon completing the questionnaire.

QA. asks whether there is a request to delay (stay) the proceedings in order to try and reach a settlement between the claimant and defendant.

QB. asks which 'Track' is considered most suitable for the case to heard. Three choices are given, the 'small claims'; the 'fast track' or the 'multi track'.

QC. asks whether 'pre-action protocols' have been attempted if required. pre-action protocols at present are only required for claims relating to personal injury and clinical (formerly known as medical) negligence.

Although the aforementioned two protocols are those specifically stated at present the court practice directions regarding protocols clearly indicate that the court will expect the claimant and defendant/s to have entered into the 'spirit' of the protocols by exchanging information with the hope of generally settling the matter before proceedings are begun regardless of the type of claim.

QD. asks if there has been an application to the court for a 'Summary judgement' or if one is intended to be made, along with if there is to be a claim made against someone who is not yet a party to the proceedings do you intend to ask the court for permission to do so. The summary judgement is applicable to both claimant and defendant where either party feels that the other party does not have a valid claim or defence.

To apply for a summary judgement the permission of the court is required and the submission must prove to the courts satisfaction that the other party has no real prospect of success and that there is no other reason why the case or the issue in question should be dealt with by a trial.

QE. refers to any witnesses the parties wish to bring to the hearing and briefly what facts the witness is going to bring.

QF. asks about any experts evidence to be used at the hearing asking for their name and field of expertise; whether or not both parties will use the same expert/s and whether the evidence will be given orally and if so why it is necessary.

QG. asks if there is any reason why the case needs to be heard at a specific court and the reasons why.

QH. asks whether the party is to be represented by a solicitor or counsel at the hearing, how long the case is expected to last along with any days which could not be attended by any parties to the case.

QI. relates to costs involved through legal representation.

QJ. refers to any other information such as any documentation which the court is required to take into account, whether they have been served upon the other party and when, are the content of the documentation agreed by the other party.

Finally a place for signatures and dates.

If a defence or counter claim is felt applicable the individual should seek professional advice prior to completing and returning the form to the court.

County Court claim form-N1

N1 (CPR Part 7) Claim Form

Claim Form	In the
	Claim No.

Claimant

SEAL

Defendant(s)

Brief details of claim

Value

Defendant's name and address

£

Amount claimed	
Court fee	
Solicitor's costs	
Total amount	
Issue date	

The court office at

is open between 10 am and 4 pm Monday to Friday. When corresponding with the court, please address forms or letters to the Court Manager and quote the claim number.

N1 Claim form (CPR Part 7) c.99

Printed on behalf of The Court Service

38

	Claim No.	

Particulars of Claim (attached)(to follow)

Statement of Truth

*(I believe)(The Claimant believes) that the facts stated in these particulars of claim are true.

* I am duly authorised by the claimant to sign this statement

Full name _____

Name of claimant's solicitor's firm _____

signed _____ position or office held_____

*(Claimant)(Litigation friend)(Claimant's solicitor)   (if signing on behalf of firm or company)

*delete as appropriate

Claimant's or claimant's solicitor's address to which documents or payments should be sent if different from overleaf including (if appropriate) details of DX, fax or e-mail.

39

4

The Hire Purchase Agreement

Hire purchase is defined as "goods hired in return for scheduled periodical payments to the hirer from the person hiring the goods". Ownership of the goods will pass from the hirer to the individual hiring the good, upon the last payment being made.

There are two types of hire purchase agreement:
a) Those where the retailer sells the goods to a finance company, which in turn hires them out to the hire purchaser, and
b) Those where the retailer keeps the agreement directly between themselves and the hire purchaser. In this case the retailer collects the scheduled payments on behalf of the creditor.

Termination of the hire Purchase agreement (i.e. ending the agreement).

The individual has a 'statutory right' to end the agreement at any time prior to the last payment being made. This right may be lost if the agreement is deemed to be repudiated (i.e. cancelled) following, for example, a default in payment. In this situation the creditor may choose to end the agreement via repossession.

What happens if the individual wishes to return the goods and end the agreement prior to the last payment being made?

Upon termination by the individual the amount payable will depend upon the amount already paid:
* If less than half the price as stated on the agreement has been paid

then the individual will be required to pay the difference figure between those payments made and half the agreement price, plus any arrears.

To work out the difference figure (above):
Total H.P. price divided by 2 = £X + any arrears - any payments made = difference figure.
Note- any deposit or part exchange value used when entering into the agreement counts towards the half price figure. therefore the 'any payments made' (above) needs to include this figure along with any scheduled payments.

* If more than half the price as stated on the agreement has been paid the individual can return the goods and owe nothing, excepting any arrears and any payment claimed by the hirer in respect of failing to take reasonable care of the goods. This does not include wear and tear, but equates to neglect.

Hire purchase agreements are required under the Consumer Credit Act 1974 to show the 'half' and 'one third' figures in boxes upon the actual agreement. Liability should be checked against these figures and not in terms of calculating half of all installments.

Generally the problem faced is not with the individual wishing to terminate the agreement but with the creditor terminating the agreement due to default in the payment schedule.

Termination of the agreement by the creditor.
This can occur if there is a default in the repayment schedule and not rectified at the creditors request. This is due to the fact that most agreements state that default in the repayment schedule permits the creditor to repudiate (cancel) the agreement.

If the creditor chooses to sue for the recovery of the goods based upon defaulting payment/s certain steps must be taken in ascending order (below) or the creditor may be guilty of trespass and interference.

The following steps need to be taken by the creditor:

* A default notice (termination or calling in notice) must be served upon the individual prior to any court action is taken. The notice must give details of the default, state how it can be rectified and give the debtor at least 7 days to act upon the notice received (i.e. pay the arrears stated or in some cases reach an agreement to clear the arrears via additional payments on top of the contractual payment figure). It will also need to state the consequences of non-compliance with the default notice.

A court order is needed to repossess the goods in the following situations:

A) Those goods where 'one third' of the agreement price has been paid. To establish the 'one third' price see the above equation.

B) If the creditor has to enter the individuals premises to repossess the goods a court order will be required if less than 'one third' of the agreement price has been paid. Premises although not defined would include all of the individuals property such as the driveway.

If the goods are repossessed without a court order, in A above, then the agreement is terminated and the individual is released from all and any existing liability and entitled to recover any monies paid up to and including the date the goods were repossessed

Should the creditor enter premises without the individuals permission and remove the goods, this would be trespass. If this does occur it is possible to take action through the county court and sue for damages.

No court order is needed in the following situations:

* If the individual gives permission to the creditor to repossess.

* If the goods have been abandoned, are on public ground and less than the 'one third' price has been paid.

If the creditor wishes to repossess the hired goods a 'fixed date summons' is served upon the individual (N4 /N10). If however the

42

creditor wishes to take court action for any arrears following a previous repossession or termination a 'default summons' will be issued.

Upon the court receiving the fixed date summons/reply, it can make one of the orders below:

* An 'absolute order'
This order states that the hired goods be returned to the creditor by a set date.
* A 'conditional order'
this order states the individual can retain the goods on the condition that either the contractual installments are made, plus a payment towards the arrears or on payment of the value of the goods.

With regards to the conditional order (above), termination of the agreement will be dependent upon the court order itself. For example, the order may state that upon default the conditional order is terminated immediately or upon default the creditor must make a further application to the court in respect of the matter of repossession.

Any of the orders above, if breached is enforceable via a 'warrant of delivery' (i.e. bailiffs).

In conclusion it is worth bringing to the readers attention; Disposal (gift or sale) of hired goods prior to passage of ownership to the individual is classified as 'appropriation' which is a criminal offence of theft. Also any insurance money paid in respect of hired goods, prior to passage of ownership, (i.e. H.P. vehicle written off and insurance company pays out to the individual) is due to the creditor.

As with all areas mentioned throughout this book the author cannot advise strongly enough that if problems of this nature occur seek specialist advice.

5

Negotiating with creditor/s and financial statements

As an aid to clarity a 'non priority' creditor is one that if non payment is made towards the debt, it will not jeopardise the individuals home, utility supplies, or liberty. Non priority debts, would for example include; credit cards, personal loans from a bank or finance company and most agreements under the Consumer Credit Act 1974.

Negotiating is, very, simply the process of two or more persons entering into discussions in order to reach a mutual agreement or settlement over the matter in question. This text will concentrate on the negotiations which will take place between the individual and the creditor or agent (debt collection agency / solicitor).

In the majority of cases it will be found that creditors are sensible and of a rational disposition, hoping to achieve an agreed mutual understanding of how the indebtedness is to be addressed.

When dealing with the creditor or agent, it is worth bearing in mind the following points;

* The creditor or agent should always be addressed civilly, regardless of the tone of their letters. The creditor/agent is only doing their job even though the letters received by the individual appear to be rather blunt and sometimes over demanding. This is simply business and as such the form and content of any letters received will be written in business language.

* Addressing creditors civilly and with a degree of respect does not mean that whatever the creditor suggests or rejects as a solution should be accepted, just to please the creditor.

* One of the keys to goods negotiating is to keep any emotional feelings out of the arena. Rely upon the facts and a logical, well thought through, supported plan of action.

* The aim the individual is striving for in negotiations of this nature is to resolve the problem at the lowest possible financial cost to oneself.

* The method of achieving these aims is by the individual looking at the means at his/her disposal, and without being 'dogmatic or rude', sticking to their guns.

* It is of no use to either the individual or creditor if, after an initial period of negotiations the individual agrees to a repayment schedule to pay off the debt at, say, £20 per week if there is no or little chance of the individual making these payments.

* The overriding factor is that any agreement reached between the individual and the creditor has to be beneficial to both sides, workable, sustainable and objective.

* Many times it is encountered that creditors or their agents state it is not possible to accept less than £X per week/month towards a repayment schedule based upon their internal guidelines. When faced with this response it should be remembered that 'guidelines' are exactly what they are, and not rules written on tablets of stone. Explanation from the individual as to why such a repayment cannot be met along with an offer of payment, which can be made, is the logical way forward.

As a general rule of thumb and dependent upon the age of the debt, previous contact with the creditor, previous repayment schedules which have broken down dictates the flexibility that the creditor will bring to the negotiations.

Certain creditors may be encountered that are far from rational in their response or attitude to the problem at hand. They tend to be inflexible, unrealistic, emotional, threatening and sometimes plain rude with their demands for repayment.

Do not get 'sucked into' debating or arguing over these issues. Stick to a logical base of negotiations expressed clearly and courteously.

It is very easy to totally disagree with a creditors proposal, rejection or moralistic viewpoint without the need to be rude, or disrespectful and it will always be to the individuals advantage to learn this.

Creditors in general will make observations as to why the individual can 'pay more' than is being offered. Some of the more common one's are:

* that payment towards, for example, satellite television is a luxury item that can be dispensed with therefore leaving more money to be offered towards the repayment schedule. These arguments should be discounted and ignored, as items of home entertainment including video recorders are acceptable expenditure. The only exception to the 'satellite/cable' situation being if the agreement is nearly at an end for the supply of the service, then the individual needs to assess the cost against other items of expenditure.

* The creditor may suggest that the individual is 'overspending' given the circumstances on items such as; telephone, travel (car), or life insurance expenses listed upon the financial statement. If this is encountered it is wise to be prepared to explain the necessity for the expenditure.

For example: the costs of running a car would include not simply the petrol but insurance, tax, MOT and general maintenance. The car may be required for work and public transport was not suitable or available. The telephone may be required not simply as a luxury but for emergency use, checking on elderly relatives or medical problems within the individuals household or security reasons.

- payments made towards pets is another item which will usually be brought into question especially if for example pet food is listed as a separate item and is high. There is no simply answer but you could ask the creditor what he or she suggests should be done with the pet.

- The creditor may generalise and be unmoving and simply demand more than is being offered.

In this situation strong reliance is based upon a good financial statement (below) and requesting the creditor to state where further money could be taken from.

- Certain creditors may suggest that the proposed offer especially a low one will be accepted if the individual agrees to a 'voluntary charge' on the individuals home. This should be refused outright.

The financial statement.
This can only be described as the most powerful tool in any negotiations of this nature, if it is presented clearly and correctly.

Once you have completed your budget statement (example below), ensuring you have incorporated all your essential expenditure, you simply deduct the outgoing finances from the incoming finances.

Your name and address & date.
Monthly / Weekly Income
Salary/Wages (self)
Salary/Wages (spouse)
Child Benefit

Other Benefits
Maintenance
Other
Monthly / Weekly Total.

Monthly / Weekly Outgoings
Mortgage / Rent
Council Tax
Water Rates
Endowment
Insurance's (list)
Electricity
Gas
Food
Household Items
Clothing / Footwear
TV rental
TV Licence
Telephone
Travel
School dinners
Car Tax / insurance
Health Costs
Magistrates court fines
County court judgements
Miscellaneous
Monthly / Weekly Total

Deduct total out goings from total incoming, this leaves of available income.

The above is an example of items of income /expenditure that an individual/ family may have. However you will need to tailor the above to your own situation, which only you know.

* To turn annual figures to weekly / monthly, take total figure and divide by 52(weeks) or 12(months).

* To turn quarterly figures into the above multiply by 4 and divide by 52(weeks) or 12(months).

* To turn monthly into weekly multiply figure by 12(months) and divide by 52(weeks), reverse the process for weekly into monthly.

At this point you will be faced with one of the two following scenario's:

a) There will be some spare money available after accounting for all your essential expenditure.
b) There will be no money left over.

If the latter situation is revealed then there is simply no offer to be made to the creditor excepting, if you so desire a 'token offer' of a small amount such as for example £1.00 per calendar month. If the former situation is revealed it may be possible to make some form of offer of payment, this does not necessarily mean the full contractual repayment, which is required.

If there is only one creditor then the mathematics are straightforward, however if there is more than one creditor then a 'fair offer' is normal. For example;

Lets assume you have three creditors A, B and C. The amount outstanding to each is; A-£600.00 B-£250.00 C-£400.00

After working out your budget statement you find that you have £24.00 per week spare.

The simply equation for finding out how much should or could be offered to each individual creditor on a fair basis is;

Take sum total of money available (£24.00) multiplied by the individual debt (A, B or C) divided by the total amount owed to all creditors (£600+250+400=1250.00). The answer is the 'fair offer'.

E.g. 24.00 * (A) 600.00 = 14400 divided by (A, B&C) 1250.00 = £11.52

24.00 * (B) 250.00 = 6000 divided by (AB&C) 1250.00 = £ 4.80

24.00 * (C) 400.00 = 9600 divided by (A, B&C) 1250.00 = £ 7.68

(* = multiply or times)

The total of the 'fair offers' = £24.00, which exactly matches your spare weekly money.

The above as stated is the fair way to allocate any available monies to more than one creditor.

It also needs noting that when talking about essential expenditure a very basic explanation can be presented to aid clarification.

Essential expenditure is that expenditure which is more important than other expenditure, therefore it stands to reason that the mortgage or rent is vitally essential as if you do not pay you are likely to be evicted and loose the roof above your head.

Equally there are other such expenditures for example utilities (gas, electric, water rates and local taxation-council tax).

There are alternatives to the straightforward offer via a repayment schedule proposal, as outlined below.

The 'write off '.
This is a request to the creditor that the debt in question is not pursued and deleted from the company records.

This route could be pursued by the individual if there is no available income to make any offer to the creditor, based upon a financial statement and personal circumstances of the individual.

For example: if the individuals personal and financial circumstances show that there are no realisable assets (i.e. no property or goods of value), the income of the individual is low or solely reliant upon state benefit/s, the financial situation is static and has been so for some time, the prospects of it improving in the foreseeable future is nil.

If this route is taken the above areas will need to brought to the attention of the creditor in the letter requesting the actual 'write off'. In addition, if the individual has more than one debt, which is not uncommon, the total indebtedness should be brought to the creditors attention.

Creditors will always have a policy related towards 'writing debts off ' based upon the cost of recovering the debt, the age of the debt, any previous recovery action which has been attempted, the success rate of any future recovery action such as issuing a summons or bankruptcy for example. If the creditor can, from details provided (above), see that recovery action is futile the chance of a 'write off ' is always possible regardless of the size of the debt.

However do not expect the creditor to simply 'throw in the towel' immediately, as the initial request is often refused. It is customary practice that nil payments will be accepted for a period of time (usually 3-6 months) at which point the situation will be reviewed. If at the end of this period the individuals circumstances remain unchanged, simply reiterate the former request for a 'write off '.

If the creditor agrees to 'write off ' the debt, then confirmation, in writing, needs to be obtained from the creditor. This is because some creditors may infer that the debt has been 'written off ' where in fact it is merely 'shelved' to be re-opened at a later date.

The full and final settlement

This is an offer to repay the debt in part by offering a lump sum payment to the creditor with the creditor agreeing to write off the remainder of the debt.

How does it work?
Very simply negotiations take place inviting the creditor to accept a lump sum of £X and agree to write the rest of the debt off. Negotiations take place by letter and accompanying financial statement.

Will it work?
This all depends upon the creditor, his thought pattern and your financial circumstances at present, your future prospects and the sum being offered along with the debts age and the length of time the creditor has been trying to recoup the debt.

Lets look at the following example:
Mr & Mrs K had their house repossessed, after sale there was a shortfall owing to the building society of 23,000. Mr & Mrs K have three children, live in local authority housing with no assets and Mr K is in a low paid job in the local factory. After taking into account their priority expenditure there is little left over to pay the debt. For whatever reason there is a £1,000 lump sum available to offer to the creditor in a full and final settlement. The offer is made.

Will it be accepted and what is the creditor thinking?
The simple answer is no, but don't be disheartened. Like any businessman the first offer is always likely to be rejected on the thought basis that more money is in reality available along with the fact that negotiations have only just begun and therefore the individual will increase the offer. The trick is to stick to your guns and re-iterate your offer and not be pressurised or put off by the initial refusal.

Other thoughts that will be running through the creditors mind:
* Lets suggest our own offer, which will be on the high side and open

to negotiation, and see if it will be met.
* Let's prolong the negotiations and threaten court action or hand it over to a debt collection agency.
* Let's issue a county court summons and sue them.

In respect of the former two it is sometimes a tactic to get the offer increased and apply pressure and may well be taken. It is simply the case of as above stated sticking to your guns and re-iterating the offer either to the creditor direct or debt collection agency. It is sometimes helpful to explain why the offer you have made is the best you can make and why.

The third option, that of suing you. Apart from the threat and pressure that is brought to bear in as much as the average every day person thinks they are going to have to attend a court full of be-wigged judges, jurors and ushers which is far from reality, the creditor is going to be well aware of your financial circumstances by this time and the nominal amount of available income you have. His mind works in figures for example:

To issue the county court summons the court fee alone, for this sum, is £100.00. This is not including solicitors fees if one is used. Lets assume he uses Cheap Sue & CO' Solicitors and their fee is £20.00.

The total amount claimed on the summons will be £23,120. excluding statutory interest. Upon receipt you complete the admission part of the summons (see appendix f) offering £1.00 per calendar month which is quite permissible if your finances dictate that is all you can afford. On this example it is going to take the creditor 120 months or 10 years to recoup the court fees and solicitors costs alone.

Suddenly the £1,000 seems awfully attractive

The above example of Mr & Mrs K can now be compared with the following scenario of Mr & Mrs L. based upon negotiating a full and final settlement.

"Mr & Mrs L. through no fault of their own fell on hard times (loss of job, reduction in overtime, etc.) for whatever reason and have a joint debts of £10,000. The situation has now improved and both Mr & Mrs are working in good jobs and finances are looking up but after taking account of priority expenditure they cannot meet the contractual payment to service the debt. They own their own home and there is a small amount of equity in it."

The full and final settlement offer that the L's will have to put forward will need to be higher than the K's (above) and more tempting to the creditor than the alternatives below.

The basic rule of thumb in considering a figure, which may be accepted in full and final settlement if there are alternative options for the creditor to pursue, is start at the bottom, which is 33% of the debt. However with every full and final settlement the final offer is based upon and dictated by the individuals financial circumstances. Do not therefore assume any figure less than a third will necessarily be rejected.

The main reason why the figure in respect of the full and final settlement is larger is due to the fact that the creditor if they so choose can use the court to enforce the debt which may be to their advantage in the long term and may apply for an 'Attachment of Earnings order', 'Charging order', 'Garnishee order' or 'Warrant of Execution' if there is a county court judgement in place and in default. However if the judgement does not fall into default then non of the aforementioned can be applied for. It could even give consideration to making the L's bankrupt. Once again the creditor will be considering the situation of 'a bird in the hand may be worth two in the bush'.

Lets consider the following example: the L's creditor in his infinite wisdom decides to issue court proceeding and they are served with a county court summons. They complete it and after addressing

addressing all priority expenditure can afford a hefty payment of £50.00 per calendar month. Based upon the above costs off issuing the summons lets assume the total claimed, excluding statutory interest is

£10,120. If everything runs to plan the creditor should receive full payment in 202 months or 16 years 8 months.

Once again it can be seen why the creditor may feel a full and final settlement looks an attractive proposition and putting the remaining sum written off down as a tax loss against profits in his end of year accounts.

What to do if the creditor agrees to your lump sum offer.
Yes jump for joy is one answer, but on a practical note the following should be adhered too;
* never pay any money over until you have a letter of agreement from the creditor which is signed by him.
* always check the wording to make sure it is exactly what has been agreed.

Before you pay any money it is wise to bear in mind the principles under the law of contract which is 'that partial payment of the whole is not legally binding because an offer to do something less than that which is already contracted to be done does not provide the required consideration to make a valid contract'.

This why the following information will safeguard you and will depend where your lump sum is coming from (i.e. you or a third party) and whether the offer of a full and final settlement is made to one or all creditors.

* If a single creditor or some of your creditor and funds are coming from you, a deed is required. It suddenly sounds all technical but any solicitor can draw one up.

* If it is all your creditors and the funds are coming from you, a letter as above mentioned will suffice.

* If the funds are coming from a third party, whether it be to a single creditor, some or all, a letter as above mentioned will again suffice.

* If the debt is a mortgage shortfall, a deed.

6
The Statutory Demand

What is it, why is it served and what can be done about it?

This is a legal document sent to the debtor, by the creditor not the court, as a final warning to pay the debt due or the creditor will, or may, petition for the debtors bankruptcy.

The creditor can only petition for the debtors bankruptcy if the debt is unsecured and for a fixed sum for which the debtor 'appears unable to pay'. The term 'appears to be unable to pay' can be satisfied in two ways:

A) When a statutory demand has been served upon the debtor and payment of the debt is not made, or
B) A county court judgement has been previously obtained against the debtor and enforcement of that judgement has been unsuccessful via the use of bailiffs because the warrant of execution has been returned unsatisfied.

In the latter there is no requirement for the creditor to issue a statutory demand before petitioning the debtors bankruptcy. There is no necessity for the creditor to issue any court proceedings prior to issuing a statutory demand. The only criteria the creditor must satisfy prior to issuing the demand is:

* The debtor must owe the creditor £750.00 or more and the debt be unsecured and for a fixed sum. More than one creditor can 'join together' to meet the £750.00 requirement.

If the statutory demand has been correctly served, the debtor has 21 days from the date of service (date the debtor received it) to do one of six things to prevent the creditor petitioning for the debtors bankruptcy.

A) pay the amount claimed.
B) offer to secure the debt against property via a voluntary charge.
C) make an offer to repay the debt via installments agreed to by the creditor.
D) bring the debt below £750.00 (i.e. pay off some of the amount).
E) enter into an individual voluntary arrangement.
F) set the demand aside, if possible.

Setting aside the statutory demand.

To set aside the statutory demand the debtor must make an application within 18 days of the date of service of the demand supported by a sworn affidavit. It is possible to apply after the 18-day period but a time extension must be asked for along with the reasons for the request). Both forms of applications are submitted in the same way and presented to:

A) The Royal Courts of Justice if resident within the London borough.
B) The county court where the debtor would petition for their own bankruptcy.
C) If due to non-payment of a county court judgement, the court the judgement was issued at.

The courts decision.

Once the application is received the court will consider the submission (neither party, debtor or creditor, will be present at this stage) and decide one of two things:

A) dismiss the application and grant the creditor permission to issue the bankruptcy petition, or
B) fix a date for a hearing if the court feels the debtor has shown

'sufficient cause' (i.e. has a reasonable ground for setting the demand aside).

If in 'B' the debtor must be present at the hearing. At the hearing and based upon the debtors application and sworn affidavit the court may set the demand aside if;

A) The creditor appears to hold some security for the debt and that security equals or exceeds the full amount of the debt.

B) The debtor disputes the debt and the reasons for the dispute appear to the court to be reasonable.

C) The debtor appears to have 'counterclaim', which equals or exceeds the amount of the debt claimed by the creditor.

D) The court is satisfied based upon other grounds, for example;

* the demand was issued in error (debt secured or less than £750.00).

* a reasonable offer of repayment or security has been turned down.

* the debtor can demonstrate that they are not insolvent and can pay the debt.

* or upon other alternatives which may be deemed more appropriate (i.e. IVA, AO).

Note - The court cannot set aside the statutory demand based upon the fact that the debtor can pay the debt at some future date.

Creditors sometimes use the statutory demand to put pressure upon the debtor to enter into a repayment schedule without ever the intention of petitioning the debtors bankruptcy. It is usual in these cases for the creditor to have the demand 'posted' to the debtor. If however the demand is served 'personally' upon the debtor this is unlikely to be a 'collection technique' hoping for a repayment arrangement schedule suggestion but the 'real thing' (i.e. the bankruptcy petition will follow).

As a final note all statutory demands should be taken seriously and acted upon immediately by contacting the creditor or creditors agent, (solicitor), making an application to set aside the demand and/or seeking further advice.

7

The Administration Order (A.O.)

What is it?

These are orders made by the county court amalgamating all your debts and allowing you to make one payment into the court each month. The court then distributes this payment on a pro-rata basis to (fairly amongst) all the creditors listed on the A.O.

You will usually have to pay the whole amount of the debt, however the court can make a percentage A.O. known as a 'Composition Order' which means that only a proportion of the debt is repaid and the remainder written off (see below). Whilst the A.O. is in place no further action can be taken by the creditor against you.

Pre-requisite criteria

To be able to apply for an A.O. You must have at least two debts one of which must be under a county court judgement and the total debts added together must be not more than £5,000.

Who can apply for an A.O.

You as an individual. It is not possible for husband and wives etc. to apply for a joint A.O. each must make their own individual application even if there are joint debts (see below).

How do I apply for an A.O.

The application is a simple process of filling out a court form N92 available free of charge from any county court office.

accompanied by details on how to complete the A.O. There is equally no court fee to submit the application.

Completing the N92.

Read the accompanying instructions. This may sound obvious but it is surprising how many individuals just 'scan' instructions and do not really digest the content before beginning.

Get two copies of the N92, either at the court office or photocopy the one you have. Basic human nature dictates that whoever you are after reading the instruction you will start entering names, dates, debts and figures only to realise half way through the form that you have ticked the wrong box, inserted the wrong figure/s or miss-spelt a creditors name. Use the first one as your draft copy making any deletions and / or corrections necessary and when you are satisfied it is correct copy the details onto the form you are going to submit to the court. Forms presented clearly and without amended deletions command more respect.

Enter the details in block capitals preferably in black ink. Once you have completed the form make a copy of it for yourself.

When entering the name of the county court on your application, this is your local county court, which may be different to the county court named on the judgement you have.

When completing your creditor list on the form make sure you enter the creditors name, address and the account number. If the account has been handed over to a solicitor or debt collection agency enter their name and address as well. For example;

J. Bloggs Mail Order Co': 3 Mail-order Lane, Anytown. Account number 11221132 (In the hands of: Debt Collectors & Co', Debiting Road, Anytown. Account number 11221132. If the account number is different insert the one applicable to the debt collection agency)

What do I do when the A.O. has been completed?

You take the completed, unsigned, form with attached judgement and covering letter, if necessary, to your local county court together with proof of your debts, and a financial statement although this will be included in the form itself. The form will then be signed by you in front of an officer of the court swearing upon oath that the information set down in your application is true. There is no fee payable for this, however the oath and signing can take place in front of any solicitor but he or she is likely to charge you a fee for this.

What does the court do when they receive my application for the A.O?

The full order

Upon receipt court staff will make a determination as to whether the total debts can be repaid within a 'reasonable time' (the term "reasonable time" is between 3 and 5 years, 3 years being the norm). If the total debt can be repaid in this 'reasonable time' the court staff will set a proposed rate of payment based upon your offer and/or guidelines set down by the Lord Chancellors office. Once this has been done the proposed rate of the payment calculated will be sent to all creditors on the order and you.

This is done to allow any of the parties involved to make objections to the order being made. Creditors may object to the proposed rate of payment or their inclusion in the A.O. itself. You may object to the proposed rate of payment set, if it differs from your original offer.

If the court receives no objections within 16 days the A.O. is made final, in other words it is set up as the proposals state.

If there any objections then a hearing before a district judge will be set to listen to the objections. If it is that a creditor has objected the district judge will make a decision whether to grant the A.O. (i.e. make it a final order) or not.

As a general rule unless the information on the application form is incorrect or the making of the A.O. would unreasonably deny the creditor taking another remedy, the order will usually be made.

It should be noted that even if creditors object they rarely attend the hearing but rely on written objections and the majority of creditors do not even object.

If it is that the total debt cannot be paid within a 'reasonable time' the court staff will pass the application over to a district judge who will make a decision on the matter. The district judge can propose the repayment period is extended to pay the full debt or make a 'Composition Order' without the need for a hearing or alternatively may set a date for a hearing of the order.

Once again notification of this is sent to all parties including you for any objections to be received within the 16 day period, or 14 days notice will be given as to the date of the hearing if one is to be set.

It is hopefully understood that the above 'Full Order' in respect of an A.O. means you can repay the full debt over a reasonable time (i.e. 3years). Lets now look at the 'Composition Order'.

The Composition Order (C.O.)

What is it?
Very simply a C.O. is an A.O. which stipulates that you only repay a proportion of your debt with the rest being written off. These are normally automatically considered by the court when the A.O. would take longer than a ' reasonable time' to be discharged. However some courts may not automatically consider a C.O. unless it is brought to their attention, it is therefore imperative that on the application form (N92) it should be requested, or alternatively attach a covering letter requesting a C.O. be considered.

How does it work?

This will be explained by example. Mr. E. has a total debt of £4,500 split between 4 creditors:

* Biffies Bank plc £1,250; Clowns Credit & CO' £750.00; Gastros Emporium £2,100; Misty Mail order £400.00.

After completing his financial statement Mr. E. has £30.00 per calendar month of spare income which he can offer on his A.O. application.

36 months (3 years) multiplied by £30.00 = £1080 this is the total amount to be paid over the 3 years on the C.O. less the courts administrative charge of 10% = £108.00. Therefor the total amount going to the creditors will be £1080 - £108.00 = £972.00.

£972.00 multiplied by 100 and divided by the total debt of £4,500 equals the percentage in the pound which will be paid to the creditors. The percentage figure being 21.6%.

By the end of the C.O. (3 years); Biffies bank will have received £270.00; Clowns Credit & CO' £162.00; Gastros Emporium £453.60 and Misty mail order £ 86.40.

On Mr.E's A.O. application requesting a C.O. be considered, he can insert in box 9 of the form that he can pay £30.00 per month, which is 26.6pence in the pound.

What happens if the A.O. is granted either in 'Full' or in 'Composition'?

You will receive notification of the order as set along with the monthly payment which is to be paid to the court and by what date in each month (see appendix c).

Upon receipt of your monthly payments the court takes control of the distribution of the money paid to the creditors. The payments are made every 3 months or when 10% of the debt has been paid into the court, which ever comes first. The A.O. is reviewed quarterly to make sure that your payments to the court have been maintained.

How and when does the A.O. end?
The A.O. ends when all debts have been paid in full (if Full Order) or the proportion as set down under the C.O., by the court, have been paid.

When the A.O. has been paid in 'Full' you can request from the court a 'certificate of satisfaction' (there is a £3.00 fee to pay for this). The court will then notify the Register of County Court Judgements that the A.O. has been paid. Any county court judgement which was included in the A.O. can equally be marked as 'satisfied' (fully paid). There is a separate fee for this and applies to each judgement.

If it is a C.O. and has been fully paid. The above 'certificate of satisfaction' can be applied for and noted at the registry against the A.O. but any individual judgements included in the A.O. will not be able to be marked as 'satisfied' because they have not been fully paid.

What happens if the A.O. has been running for a while and I can't keep up with the payments because my financial circumstances have changed?
You can ask the court to review the A.O. (as can any of your creditors and the court itself) by applying to the court by letter or court form N244 (see appendix d) setting out the reasons why the review is requested. If it is because your finances have been reduced a new financial statement showing your new income and expenditure should be attached.

Upon receipt of your application, regardless of whether it is a 'Full' A.O. or Composition in place, the court has the power to:
* Order the monthly payment to be reduced.
* Order a complete suspension of payments for a set period of time (i.e. no payments).
* Make a C.O. if one was not initially granted.

Can I apply for a C.O. even if one was not initially granted and an A.O. is in place?

Yes this is possible, giving it between 6 and 12 months from the initial order, by making an application on form N244. A hearing date will be set and it is the reasons you give as to the chances of the C.O. being granted, along with any objections of the creditors.

The following are some points that you could bring to the attention of the district judge:

* Guidance from the Lord Chancellors department regarding an A.O. is that 3 years is a reasonable time for it to run.
* If a composition order is refused the A.O. would run on for some considerable time and offer 'no light at the end of the tunnel'.
* Creditors are protected from positive changes in your financial situation in as much as they can ask for a review of the order and your financial situation to see if the installments can be increased, if for example your income increases substantially
* Bankruptcy would only have lasted 2 years if either you or the creditor had taken that route.
* Many creditors can offset tax and V.A.T losses against profits rather than receiving small sums over a long period of time.

What happens if I miss payments

Apart from being ill advised. If you miss two or more consecutive payments and / or regularly fail to make payment to the court on time, the court should contact you over the matter instructing you to do one of the following;

* To make the payments due
* Give an explanation for your reason of non payment
* Set out your proposals to repay the arrears
* Make an application for a variation of the order (N.244 as above)

If you respond, which is wise that you do, the response will be given to a district judge who has the discretion in the matter and may:

* Order a hearing of the matter * Revoke or suspend the order * Vary the order

If the order is revoked (i.e. cancelled) the court will no longer accept your payments and will inform all creditors that they are free to pursue there debts via alternative actions if they choose.

If you do not respond within 16 days to the courts request, the order will be revoked.

If the order is revoked creditors in general appear not to pursue the debt. However there is no guarantee especially if they are a creditor with a county court judgement in place against you.

If the order is revoked because of non payment and after a time you find you are now in the position to clear the arrears or a substantial part of them and continue with the originally ordered payments it is possible to request the court re-instate the A.O.

Using Tactics
If you are just over the £5,000 limit consider the following:
* One of the standard methods of keeping below the limit is to exclude certain priority debts from the A.O. by including any arrears payments as normal expenditure. For example you have electricity arrears and have come to an arrangement with the Electricity company to repay the arrears at £x on top of your normal usage, simply list this in your expenditure list.

* Do not include creditors where there is a dispute over liability (i.e. how much is owed or any flawed consumer credit agreement).
* If the A.O. route looks favourable but you do not have a county court judgement it may be worth encouraging a creditor to take action.
* If there is one county court judgement in place but is in joint names, the same judgement can be used to make separate A.O. applications by one or both people named upon the judgement.

KEY ADVICE GUIDES-THE DEBTORS HANDBOOK

General notes on Administration Orders

* When calculating the total debt to see if it falls within the limit set down (£5,000) make sure all your debts are included. If there has been an oversight and a new creditor needs to be added to the A.O. which is possible, given the surrounding circumstances leading to the application it is best to seek further advice.

• Although all debts should be calculated regarding the £5,000 limit only arrears of the following need to be included, Hire Purchase agreements, Community Charge (Poll Tax), Council Tax; Maintenance and Child Support debts.

* Only individual applications for A.O. are permissible even if for example a husband and wife have a joint debt/s

* Joint debts are generally unable to be split 50/50. However if for example both husband and wife are applying for an A.O. in their own right at the same time it may be possible to split the total debt or alternatively list it on one of the applications and make a note on the other that the debt in question is included in the other application. This all depends upon the local court practice in the area you are applying to and so there is no hard and fast answer other than check with the court before submitting the application.

* If it is that one of the couple enter the whole joint debt on their A.O. and the other leaves it off as above the creditor is quite within their rights to pursue the other for the debt.

* When an A.O. has been granted any creditor listed on the A.O. can apply to the court for any of the applicants assets which have a value of £50.00 or more to be seized, sold and the proceeds brought to the A.O. However this, in practice, rarely ever occurs.

* If you can afford to make an offer of payment in box 9 it should be inserted, however if no offer is able to be made, due to no available

spare income, then the space in box 9 should be left blank. The figure will then be inserted by the court based on a calculation of means.

* In box 9 there is a question relating to an attachment of earnings (see appendix c) it is wise to tick this and state your reasons as required. Good reasons are that an attachment of earnings may jeopardise your position of employment (i.e. you might get sacked).

* An A.O. application can be refused upon the district judges discretion if it is felt that the debts have occurred through recklessness or irresponsibility, or if you have large assets or other securities that could be sold to discharge a substantial part of the debts but you refuse to do so. This however does not include the home.

* An A.O. application may be turned down if the information you have provided on the form indicates that you do not have enough money to meet the monthly payment offered.

* There is nothing to stop you attaching separate financial statements and other relevant notes which may make things clearer than on the actual A.O. application form. However it is to be noted that this additional information must accompany a fully completed A.O. application form.

* If you on a low income and have very little money when making the offer on the A.O. or are reliant solely upon state benefits an offer of between £1.00-£5.00 per month is quite acceptable. Do not make the mistake of offering more than you can afford or thinking your offer is too low.

The Advantages and disadvantages of A.O's.

Advantages
* Creditors cannot take any further enforcement action whilst the A.O. is in force.
* Debts can be partially written off if a composition order is granted

* Interest on all debts is frozen
* All creditors are treated fairly
* You only have to make one monthly payment to the court
* Any variation of the order regarding payments only involves dealing with the court
* It avoids the problem of dealing with lots of debts and independent creditors
* It is a cheap way of dealing with debts
* It is a quicker way of negotiating payments

Disadvantages
* The court charges a fee for the A.O.
* You must have one County Court Judgement against you
* The court may not agree to a composition order
* You may have to attend the court
* There is a £5,000 limit
* The A.O. does not prevent a creditor from pursuing bankruptcy but they will need leave (permission) of the court to do so if the total debt does not exceed £1,500.
* Some district judges have been known to treat a mortgage as a debt, whether it be in arrears or not, thus taking the total debt over the limit.

8

The Individual Voluntary Arrangement (I.V.A)

What is it?
Very basically an IVA is a method of addressing and eventually discharging an individuals total indebtedness based upon an arrangement made between the debtor and the creditors to repay a % of the debt over a period of usually 3 - 5 years, under the watchful eye of an insolvency practitioner without the need to go down the bankruptcy route and its inherent / related problems.

Pre-requisite conditions
Before going further it may be worth while considering if there are any pre-requisite conditions to be satisfied before an individual can consider this route. The short answer is yes and that is there must be some available income and / or cash lump sum that can be brought to the IVA. and you must not have had an I.P. make application, on your behalf for an interim order to the court within the preceding 12 months (further details below).

E.G. H&W have £15,000 worth of debt. They have a monthly available income of £200.00 after addressing all priority creditors. H&W can therefor bring an offer to the IVA of £200.00pcm.

However this is not to say that a smaller monthly figure would jeopardize the possibility of considering an IVA.

E.G. H&W have £25,000 worth of debt, have £80.00 pcm available income. Initially this is all H&W can bring to the IVA. However maybe W is going to return to work and this figure would be increased or

H&W have an asset that when sold will be brought to the IVA. The IVA should not be excluded based solely upon a small monthly figure of available income alone.

Is it possible for me to enter into an I.V.A.?
In the majority common sense plays a large role in considering the possible success of any IVA proposal based upon considerations such as;

* Creditors will be looking to receive upwards of between 20 - 30% of the total debt over the five years. (that is not to say that a lower % than 20 is not worth considering)
* The IP will either want his fees paid up front or the fee will be incorporated into the IVA and taken from the payments made as a %.
* The individual will need to be able to stick to the arrangement, mentally, physically and monetary. Five years is a long time and can be psychologically draining.

Can I enter into an I.V.A. if;
* One of my creditors is or has threatened to make me bankrupt and have already received a 'statutory demand'?......Yes.
* A bankruptcy order has already been made against me?.......Yes.
* I am a self employed?.......Yes.
* I am in a business partnership?.......Yes
* I am in a relationship but not all debts are joint. Can we enter into an I.V.A together?....Yes.

Is it therefore possible to pinpoint with any degree of accuracy whether an individual could look towards an IVA as a method of dealing with his/her indebtedness?
One of the largest operators in the field of managing IVA's give indications that if the total indebtedness is £10,000 + and three creditors or more and there is something to be brought to the proposal regarding a repayment schedule then it is worth a serious consideration. This does not mean that a figure below £10,000 is not considered. Obviously £5,000 and below would come under A.O.'s.

So what steps have to be taken and how does it all work?

The Initial Steps.

The first requirement is that the individual approaches an insolvency practitioner in order to discuss the possibilities of entering into an IVA. In order to assess the viability of such a request the IP will require certain information from the individual. This information consists of:

a) Brief background of the events that led up to the level of debt to be addressed.

b) A full and accurate financial statement, setting out your income and expenditure

c) A list of all your assets (if any) and their value

d) A list of all your liabilities (i.e. your debts)

e) A list of any guarantors

f) Brief proposal of how it is to be run

(i.e. The total debt being brought to the agreement is £X, to be discharged over a period of 5 years by payment of £X per month to the 'nominee / supervisor of the I.V.A.. The total payment over the above period to total £X out of which the I.P's fees are to be taken (unless they are being paid up front). If at this stage you know the fees that will be payable to the I.P. it will be possible to work out the percentage in the £ that each creditor will get (see calculation under A.O's above).

g) The reasons why the creditors may accept the proposal

(i.e. an arrangement of this nature usually produces more for the creditor than going down the bankruptcy route).

h) List any assets which you do not want to be included in the arrangement, which for most is, if possible the house, or tools/equipment if in business.

The proposals.

These should contain as much information as possible The headings above make up the base for the IP's assessment of the individuals chances of success and whether the IP will take on the case. It is generally thought that the individual should make the proposals, however ' don't panic' it is more common that the IP based upon the above information provided by the individual and further enquiry's during an initial interview will draw up the final proposal.

The proposal itself is quite a detailed document and needs to contain at its minimum; (try footnote Ins' Act 1986-section)

* The nature and amount of the individuals liabilities.
* The individuals assets and estimated value.
* Information regarding any charging orders and the extent of the charge.
* Any assets which are to be excluded from the arrangement and to what extent.
* Details of any properties excluding those owned by the individual to be included in the arrangement.
* How any associates of the individual are to be treated within the arrangement.
* The proposed length of the arrangement.
* Details of any transactions under value that the individual may have made.
* Any third party guarantees.
* Proposed dates of distribution of monies to creditors.
* How the fees to the nominee/supervisor are to be paid.
* How the funds will be dealt with
* Supervisors bank details
* If the individual is in business, how it will be run during the period of the arrangement
* If any credit will be allowed during the arrangement
* Any functions to be carried out by the supervisor
* Name and address of the supervisor and their qualifications

* There will probably be a legacy clause included into the proposals just in case you receive an inheritance, win the pools or lottery prior to the expiry of the arrangement.
* There will usually be a contingency clause dealing with matters like what happens if you are of work for a while due to sickness for example and cannot meet the scheduled payments.

It is therefore safe to assume that even with the best will in the world the average individual contemplating entering into an arrangement would be hard pressed to complete a thorough proposal without the aid of an IP. However the more information that can be provided at the initial interview can only aid the individuals initial proposal.

If after the interview and any further investigation the IP decides an arrangement as proposed is workable what happens next?
Although the proposal as above described will generally be formulated by the IP, it has to be formally served on the IP. In other words two copies of the proposal are sent to the IP for his approval, if it is accepted, the IP will sign one copy and return it to the individual at which point the IP becomes the individuals 'nominee'. In layman's language there is a professionally qualified person, an insolvency practitioner, who by putting his or her name to it is basically stating the proposal put forward will or at least should work in their professional opinion.

What happens if the proposal, as above, is accepted?
The 'nominee' (I.P) will make an application to the County Court for an 'Interim Order'. Upon receipt of the application the court will set a hearing date to hear the proposals, which may be in summary form at this stage or final if the 'nominee' has prepared them prior to the application for the interim order or during the period leading up to the hearing. It will be the nominee who attends the hearing.

If the court is satisfied based upon the 'nominees' submissions that this is a serious and workable proposal and there has been no previous proposal made within the preceding 12 months along with the undertaking that the ' nominee' is willing to act for you the 'interim order will be granted.

The order lasts for a period of 14 days, which gives the 'nominee' time to prepare the full report (if it has not already been done at the above hearing) based upon the proposals and put before the court. This must happen at least two days prior to the ending of the interim order. The report, based upon an evaluation of the proposals, states whether it is a workable solution and is worth convening a creditors meeting (see below) An extension of time can be applied for if it is required.

Whether or not the 'nominee' makes an immediate request for the 'interim order' will depend upon considerations regarding any enforcement action by creditors that is imminent, as once the interim order is granted it prevents creditors from continuing with or starting any new action against you (i.e. applying for a 'warrant of execution' and sending the bailiffs round or starting bankruptcy proceedings for example).

Accompanying the above proposal will be an affidavit (i.e. a sword statement just like the oath mentioned under the AO procedure above). Your affidavit will include;

* The reasons why you are making the application.
* You are either an undischarged bankrupt or you are able to make your own petition for bankruptcy.
* Details of any legal action that, to your knowledge, has been taken against you (i.e. any county court judgements for example) through the courts.
* There has been no previous application for an interim order made by you or on your behalf in the previous 12 months period ending at the date on your affidavit.

* The 'nominee' is qualified to act as an I.P. (i.e. she or he is an Insolvency Practitioner).
* The fact that the I.P., in question, is willing to act for you in respect of your proposal.

If you are thinking by this stage it all sounds very complicated and to some degree confusing do not panic!, it is unless, that is, you are an insolvency practitioner. That is why the very nature of the beast dictates that an I.P. has to act for you and you can not simply go ahead and do it all yourself.

In many ways once you have put together your initial proposals, had an interview with an I.P., served the proposal upon the I.P. and they have been accepted you take, for the want of a better expression, a back seat to a certain extent.

What happens once the interim order has been granted?
The I.P. will arrange for a place and time that the creditors meeting will be held. This will be between 14-28 days from the date the I.P. submitted the report to the court.

Notification off the meeting will be sent to all creditors, along with;
* Your financial statement.
* A copy of the proposals.
* The I.P's report upon the proposals.
* Proxy forms (for completion by those creditors who do not wish to attend or cannot attend the meeting)
* A statement giving details to the creditors of voting criteria (see below)

You will also be notified of the meeting because your attendance will be required.

The creditors meeting.
At the creditors meeting a vote will be held, requesting the creditors to accept or decline the proposals as discussed. To be accepted, a 75% 'yes' vote needs to be achieved. This 75% majority in 'value' not by individual numbers.
(i.e. Creditors listed and amounts owed: A=£2,000, B:=£10,000, C=£3,500, D=£2,500. If A and D decline but B and C accept, the vote is carried (Total debt £18,000 * 75% = £13,500) and binds all creditors listed, even those creditors who chose not to vote or were opposed to the proposals put forward.)

Once accepted the outcome is reported to the creditors and the court. At this point the I.V.A. is actually in place and from then on supervised by an Insolvency practitioner for its duration, ensuring the individual debtor sticks to the proposals as agreed.

If during the life time of the I.V.A. the individuals circumstances change there is always the possibility that the original proposals can be modified to account for the change, but this would have to be put before another creditors meeting. In the alternative, if the individual debtor fails to keep to the I.V.A. the Insolvency practitioner or any one of the creditors to the agreement will probably petition for the individuals bankruptcy.

Having outlined the I.V.A. procedure. the question which usually follows, is; 'can I enter into one'?

It has to be said that there are no 'hard and fast' criteria set down in order to consider entering into an I.V.A. Each one considered upon the individuals circumstances in each and every case.

As a broad base guide, which is by no means definitive, the following three factors will be considered when looking at the I.V.A. as an option.

* The total indebtedness, in general, needs to be in the region of £10,000 + but there is no maximum figure. When calculating the indebtedness it is usually underestimated by the individual as opposed to over estimated given the omissions and or realisations of additional interest or penalty charges, which have accrued and been added to the original figure.

* the offer to be brought to the I.V.A. proposed. This is the amount of repayment and method of providing it. Leaving lump sum payments to one side. There will usually need to be £100 per calendar month, which can be offered as a regular monthly payment. This figure is arrived at after deducting normal monthly outgoings such as the mortgage, housekeeping and utility payments and the like which are required for the individual to cover all living expenses from the, net, monthly

income (unsecured creditors are not calculated within this figure as they will be listed upon the I.V.A.).

* the number of creditors which will be included within the I.V.A. is very often not an issue but three or more is generally preferred.

In conclusion, if it is felt that an I.V.A. is an option to the individuals indebtedness, preparation prior to the initial interview will only be to the individuals advantage. It should be noted that there is a fee charged by the Insolvency practitioner, which can be charged 'up-front' or be taken throughout the life of the I.V.A. Fee's charged vary from one Insolvency practitioner to another and as such the individual should make enquiry's relating to these.

9
Bankruptcy

Bankruptcy, what is it?
Bankruptcy is a legal method of dealing with all debts which cannot be paid and ensuring that all the assets of the debtor are realised (i.e. turned into money via sale) and shared out fairly between all creditors.

How does it occur?
There are two ways in which bankruptcy can occur and they are;
A) The debtor can petition for their own bankruptcy, or
B) The creditor or group of creditors can petition for bankruptcy of the debtor as long as the creditor is owed £750.00 or more.

This text will concentrate upon the debtor petitioning upon their own bankruptcy.

What will you need.
A) A bankruptcy petition (Form 6.27) and a statement of affairs (Form 6.28) both forms are available from any county or high court office.
B) The name of the court to which you will present your petition.
C) The bankruptcy fee and deposit. The fee presently stands at £50 and the deposit at £250. This is payable when the petition is first presented to the court. Sometimes the court may require the fee to be paid in cash.

Completing the petition and statement of affairs forms.
The bankruptcy petition (Form 6.27).
This consists of two sides and has accompanying notes. The petition is set out presumably for those who have been in business. If you have

not been in business it does not matter, simply complete the relevant parts of the form.

The statement of affairs (Form 6.28).
The statement of affairs is somewhat longer, running through ten pages (A-G), excluding the front page, which again is accompanied by a set of guidance notes (Form B44.24). There is a lot of information requested upon the form, which may not be readily available to the prospective bankrupt. This information can obviously be obtained by the individual.

Although the guidance notes are informative certain additional notes for clarification need to be brought to the readers attention regarding completion of the statement of affairs, which are;

A) At part B. All creditors have to be listed in alphabetical order.
B) At part C1. Which asks whether or not you have any bank or building society accounts and how much is in them. Before inserting any figures here note that immediately the petition is presented to the court all bank and building society accounts are frozen and you will not be able to withdraw funds. It is therefore wise to withdraw living expenses from the account, and complete this entry just, prior to presenting your petition to the court.
C) At part C2/3. Which asks you if you own a vehicle and how much it is worth. Be careful and give this some thought before entering the figure as second hand vehicles do not always equate to the value an individual would personally put on their vehicle. At C3, you are asked what else you own which is of value. If you are inserting anything in this part remember give careful thought to any figures as auction prices do not reflect the price the item cost new, nor the replacement value. Any items listed here are at risk of being taken under the control of the bankruptcy. General household furniture would not be listed.
D) At part D. This asks you whether any distress has been levied against you (i.e. Bailiffs). Be sure to mention any of these issues here.
E) Which request you note down any ' court judgements' or 'other legal process' against you (Court judgements are self explanatory for

example any County Court judgements. Other legal process would refer to, for example, liability orders for council tax).

F) At part F. This section should only really be completed if you made attempts to make arrangements with all your creditors as a whole, not arrangements made separately with individual creditors.

G) At part G. This asks you to set out your incoming and outgoing financial expenditure. Although there is a place at the end of this section for you to insert an offer it is not necessary for you to do so if there is no available income.

What to do, and what happens when you have completed the petition and statement of affairs.

You will have already found out which court is to deal with the petition, as it will be entered onto the petition itself. This is the court that the petition needs to be presented too. The court will need the original application plus two further copies of the petition and statement of affairs. If however you are petitioning in the high court only the original application will be required.

Upon attendance at the court the affidavit will be sworn before a court officer, which is free in the county court. The high court presently charges a fee of five pounds to witness the signing.

The fee and deposit will be paid and the court will either 'hear' your petition immediately or, if busy, make a time and date for your petition to be heard.

At the hearing the court can do one of four things.

A) Dismiss the bankruptcy petition.

B) Order a 'stay' in proceedings. In other words suspend the bankruptcy petition if the court feels it requires further information in respect of the application.

C) Consideration will be given towards the possibility of referring the application to an Insolvency practitioner in respect of setting up an Individual Voluntary Arrangement if the unsecured debts total twenty thousand pounds or less, assets listed in the statement of affairs total two thousand pounds or more, the individual petitioner has not been declared bankrupt within the previous five years, or if the court feels, given the circumstances, it is appropriate to do so.

Note. If you do not want an individual voluntary arrangement this should be pointed out at the hearing.

D) If the court decides that none of the above are applicable then the bankruptcy order will be made. The order takes effect immediately (i.e. once the court makes the order at the hearing you are then bankrupt).

In addition and if appropriate the court will issue a 'certificate of summary administration'. This will be deemed appropriate if unsecured debts total twenty thousand pounds or less, you have not been declared bankrupt within the previous five years or entered into an individual voluntary arrangement and the bankruptcy order being made is a result of a debtors petition only.

If no mention is made at the hearing about a 'certificate of summary administration' you should ask the court to consider issuing one as it is not possible to raise the matter at a latter date.

There are certain benefits attached to the granting of a certificate of summary administration. In general it simplifies the whole bankruptcy procedure along with keeping costs down. An 'Official receiver' (i.e. accountant employed by the government) will be appointed to administer the bankrupts affairs.

If the bankrupt complies with his/her responsibilities under the order and has not been an undischarged bankrupt at any point during the preceding fifteen years then discharge from bankruptcy will occur after two years, instead of three years which is usual for those bankruptcy's falling outside the criteria laid down under the certificate of summary administration criteria.

The hearing over, you're now bankrupt what happens next.

At this point in time you effectively lose ownership of all your property except for those items which are excluded (below). The court will notify the official receiver and give details of the bankruptcy order made, which will be, invariably, done the same day as the order is made. The court will give you the address and telephone number of the official receivers office whom you are required to contact and an appointment will be made for you that day. If an appointment that day is not possible you will be asked some basic question and informed not to use any bank/building society accounts or credit cards during the interim period. A short questionnaire will be sent to you for completion prior to the appointment relating to your financial circumstances along with a request noting other documentation, which you are required to bring to the interview.

During this interim period the official receiver will have notified any banks, building societies or credit card companies of the bankruptcy order and instructed them to freeze the account/s, along with all utility companies (i.e. gas, electric, water) and any other organisation such as for example the benefits agency.

The official receiver will also arrange for the advertisement of the bankruptcy order to be placed in the 'London Gazette' and one other newspaper of the official receivers choice, usually a local newspaper of the area. This is done so that those creditors who are not individually notified regarding the bankruptcy can contact the official receivers office and 'prove' their debt/s.

The purpose of the interview with the official receiver.

The official receiver will check that there has been a full disclosure of all assets and debts. The majority of this information will be contained within the questionnaire. The official receiver will also look to see if you can afford to make any payment towards the creditors out of your income, voluntarily or via an 'income payment order' through the court. These payments are extremely rare and even if considered appropriate by the official receiver there must be sufficient funds left for the individuals domestic needs. In brief there must be a substantial amount of available income per month, probably in excess of £100, to make it worthwhile.

The official receiver will have to (unless a CSA granted, above) investigate your financial affairs for the period before and during the bankruptcy. This will include considerations regarding any bankruptcy or other offences which may have been committed (see below). The official receiver may, report to the court but must report to the creditors regarding assets, debts and the circumstances which led to the debtors bankruptcy.

The official receiver will then set up a plan to dispose of assets to pay all, or some, of the debts.

The next stage in the process, if the official receiver deems it appropriate, will be to visit your premises.
Business premises - visits to business premises will always, usually, occur.

The official receiver will then 'take into custody' all business assets. However the debtor is permitted under the Insolvency Act to retain:
" Tools and other items of equipment, which are necessary for and used personally by the debtor in any employment, business or vocation and includes in certain circumstances vehicles"

Also any employees will be dismissed, which is usually resultant in the business closing, and all paper work relating to the business will be collected.

Residential - Visits to residential premises do not always occur.

If a visit does take place any items of value, as scheduled in the petition/questionnaire belonging to the debtor, will be 'taken into custody' by the official receiver. However the debtor, under the Insolvency Act, is permitted to retain;

"Clothing, bedding, furniture and household equipment and possessions necessary for satisfying the basic domestic needs of the debtor and his/her family in the home"
Invariably most general household items of the debtors will not be sold. However by way of example items such as antiques and new items with a re-saleable value such as hi-fi's etc. may well be taken.

Vehicles: If this is required for work purposes it may be retained unless it is of particular value in which case it would be sold permitting the debtor a reasonable replacement out of the sale proceeds. Equally if the vehicle in question is of no real value due for example age and condition then it will not be sold.

Any valuable items, as above mentioned, will be removed and sold. It is possible for the official receiver to force entry to the debtors premises and / or have any of the debtors mail redirected, if required.

During the life of the bankruptcy. (date of bankruptcy order to date of discharge)
During the bankruptcy period the debtor is faced with certain restraints and duties. Within this period it is a criminal offence to:

· obtain credit of £250 or more, either alone or with a.n.other person without disclosing the fact of the bankruptcy.
· carry on a business, directly or indirectly, in a different name to the one in which the debtor went bankrupt without disclosing to all who do business with the debtor the name in which she/he was made bankrupt.
· take part in the, direct or indirect, promotion, formation or management of a limited company without the courts permission.

In addition and during the bankruptcy period the debtor must inform the official receive of; any assets during the period must be brought to the official receivers attention within 21 days of the debtor becoming aware of the asset.

Other offences with regards to bankruptcy in general include;

- it is an offence to dispose of any property obtained on credit, in the 12 months prior to the bankruptcy petition being presented to the court.
- the making of any false statements or omissions as to material facts relating to the debtors financial circumstances in any statement.
- the failure to disclose to the official receiver all details regarding the debtors property and disposals of any such property.
- the concealment of property with a monetary worth of £500 or more or leaving the country with the above amount or more.
- fraudulently disposing of property at an undervalue in the five years prior to the bankruptcy petition being presented. This may have been done quite innocently by the debtor but if it has occurred the official receiver can, if it thought to be fraudulent and in order to reduce the assets available to the creditors to the bankruptcy:

A) make an application to the court for the transaction to be set aside if within the preceding five years the debtor was insolvent at that time and /or,
B) make application to the court regarding any transactions within a 2 year period preceding the bankruptcy petition regardless whether or not the debtor was insolvent.

How does it end - discharge.
The majority of bankruptcy orders last for a period of three years, with the exception where the bankruptcy debt is less than £20,000 and the individual has not been bankrupt or had an Individual Voluntary Arrangement in place in the previous five years, then discharge occurs after two years.

Specific issues
As we have seen once someone has been declared bankrupt all property and other assets come under the control of the official receiver with a few exceptions. The following explains in more detail specific issues that are worthy of note.

Rented property.

In general most 'residential' tenancies do not fall under the control of the official receiver due to the law as stated under the Housing Act 1988 (s 117).

'Secured Tenancies' - these will not fall under the control of the official receiver unless assignment is by any reason set out under the Housing Act 1985 (s 91(3)).

'Assured Tenancies' - these may or may not fall under the control of the official receiver and will be based upon the content and wording of the tenancy agreement itself.

'Other tenancies' - may, within the tenancy agreement, contain a clause relating to bankruptcy in as much as an 'undischarged bankrupt cannot hold the tenancy'.

In general if the tenancy can not be 'assigned' it will not fall under the official receivers control, without the official receiver seeking the courts permission. The official receiver rarely applies to the court in these circumstances. It is worthy to note that most housing association tenancies are capable of being assigned.

If the tenancy does not fall under the official receivers control the debtor usually continues as normal and continues to pay the rent and any housing benefit claim remains in place. However if the tenancy is one that does fall under the official receivers control then the tenancy is included within the bankruptcy order.

The tenancy, in simple terms, passes into the hands of the official receiver who can 'disclaim' it. If the official receiver does decide to 'disclaim' the tenancy it would mean that the bankrupt tenant has lost the right to continue living in the property. If this were to be the case it is the responsibility of the landlord to bring possession proceedings against the tenant via the county court to obtain an eviction notice.

The reasons why the official receiver may wish to 'disclaim' a tenancy could for example be based upon the fact that it is felt that the property is too large and expensive for the bankrupts needs, or the rent that is set is too high in comparison to alternative housing locally available.

However, in general practice very few tenancies are ever 'disclaimed' by the official receiver, but specialist housing advice should be sought prior to presenting the petition to the court.

Actual rent arrears at the date of the bankruptcy.
These will be included within the bankruptcy order and the landlord will be paid like any other creditor (see below).

If there are joint tenants the other person to the tenancy will be held responsible for paying the arrears, if the landlord chooses to pursue them in the normal way.

If possession proceedings are already in motion at the time of the bankruptcy petition they will continue unless the court orders otherwise. Should the hearing over possession culminate in an outright possession order being made it would appear that a 'suspended' possession order is unable to be granted by the court. This is based upon the fact that to suspend the order on condition that the tenant continues to meet the contractual rent plus an additional sum towards the arrears, which is a debt within a bankruptcy, would in effect give the landlord a 'preferential' status over and above other creditors.

However court practices vary and it is impossible to accurately state with any degree of certainty the outcome of the court granting a 'suspended' possession order.

Mortgaged property.
This will become an asset, which falls under the control of the official receiver and will be looked at as a realisable asset from which to pay out creditors.

If the home is occupied and solely owned by the bankrupt then sale will ensue with the sale proceeds being brought to the bankruptcy. This given that there is equity in the property.

However, such a simple answer in a complex area is far from adequate in as much that many properties are, for example, in a negative equity situation, or jointly owned and only one of the joint owners is bankrupt. The following is therefore an overview of the situation, which could ensue.

If there is a situation of negative equity the official receiver may decide to delay sale if there is the possibility that the passage of time will bring positive equity. If this were the case it would only be carried through if it were thought that the payments towards the mortgage would be maintained. If this route were taken by the official receiver the property would remain an asset of the bankruptcy and be sold at a latter date, even after the bankrupt has been discharged. In this case the official receiver would usually place a charging order on the property and register a caution with the land registry.

Generally the home will be sold by the official receiver with permission of the mortgage grantor. The sale can usually be delayed for 12 months from the date of the debtor being declared bankrupt if the family home is also occupied by a partner and children.

This is to give the bankrupt and family enough time to find alternative accommodation or for the partner, friend or relative to arrange finance to purchase the bankrupts share.

If sale of the property culminates on the open market it is only the bankrupts share of the sale proceeds, which is taken to the bankruptcy. The remainder is that of the joint owner.

Due to the general complexities of bankruptcy law under the Insolvency Act, add to this the additional issues under The Law of

Property Act and it is advised that specialist advice be sought regarding this particular asset.

Hire purchase goods.

The re-saleable value of any hired goods will all depend upon whether there is any equity in the goods. Hire companies, generally, will permit the debtor to retain the goods as long as the financial commitment regarding repayment is kept. This does not mean that the hire company will not be listed in the bankruptcy petition.

Due to the fact that many such issues regarding hired goods are judged upon the individual merits of each case there are no 'hard and fast' answers as to sale and / or retention by the debtor.

Tools of a trade.

The Insolvency Act provides that "such tools, books, vehicles and other items of equipment used personally by the bankrupt in and necessary for the business, vocation, occupation are exempt and can be retained by the bankrupt'.

However the official receiver can claim any exempt goods if it is felt that the re-saleable value would exceed the cost of a reasonable replacement. This is particularly true in respect of vehicles, if for example the vehicle is particularly valuable and a cheaper replacement would do.

If the official receiver were to sell the vehicle. the bankrupt could request that part of the sale proceeds be returned to enable the purchase of a cheaper vehicle, if it can be shown that the vehicle was necessary for employment or private life.

Life insurance policies.

Generally, life insurance policies have no 'surrender value' and therefore the official receiver cannot take control of them as they are not a re-saleable asset.

However if there is a surrender value the official receiver will claim them. If the bankrupt dies the payment made from the policy would fall under the official receivers control.

During the period of the bankruptcy any payment towards the policy may be continued if the policy is in place to repay a mortgage upon death. If however the policy is a simple one that is to provide financial security for a partner upon death thought will be given towards suspending payments during the life of the bankruptcy by the official receiver or cancelling the policy entirely.

Endowment policies.
Whether or not these fall under the control of the official receiver will depend upon whether the policy is 'charged' to a mortgage.

If the policy is not 'charged', they will fall under the official receivers control as an asset and be claimed. The monetary value can be released in one of two ways:

· surrendering the policy to the endowment company, or
· auctioning the policy

The length of time the policy has been up and running will dictate whether this course of action is pursued by the official receiver. Generally speaking if it has been running for a substantial time it is likely to be pursued.

Who is paid first.
Once the official receiver has claimed all saleable assets the following will be paid first out of the funds raised:
A) All bankruptcy expenses incurred by the official receivers office and/ or insolvency practitioner.
B) Expenses related to any property sale (i.e. estate agents).
C) Any income tax (PAYE) which is owed from the year prior to the bankruptcy.

D) Any income tax payable for and on behalf of subcontractors.

E) Any value added tax which is owed for a period of 6 months prior to the bankruptcy.

F) All other taxes owed (i.e. car tax) from the year prior to the bankruptcy.

G) Any national insurance contributions from the year prior to bankruptcy.

H) Any wages owed to employee's for the 4 months prior to the bankruptcy.

I) All other creditors.

It can be imagined that, unless there are substantial and valuable assets, after taking account of all payments made between A-H above the 'ordinary' creditor usually only receives a small percentage of the actual debt they are claiming.

It is a common assumption that once the bankruptcy ends all debts not paid remain unenforceable (i.e. written off). This assumption is correct with the exception of the following debts, which can still be enforced if not fully paid under the bankruptcy:

A) Court fines such as maintenance orders, child support agency payments and other orders made through the family courts.

B) Any debts included in the bankruptcy which were connected with fraud.

C) Student loans.

D) Any debts connected with or arising from personal injury claims.

E) State benefit overpayments.

F) Secured creditors.

With regards to the above and for the aid of clarity regarding enforcement after the bankruptcy ends by the above creditors, the following situation should be noted.

With regards to general enforcement actions after discharge by any of the above creditors, if this does occur it is open to the discharged bankrupt to request the courts permission not to pay the debt being pursued based upon the fact that the debtor has recently been discharged from the bankruptcy order. Unless the debt being pursued is related to fraud the court has a discretional power to grant this request.

With regards to secured creditors. Discharge from bankruptcy does not effect the rights of the secured creditor from pursuing the debt. In other words a building society to which a mortgage is owed is quite within it's right to force property sale after a bankrupt has been discharged from the bankruptcy order.

However if during the bankruptcy, or after the bankruptcy period, the home was sold by the official receiver, or a forced sale arranged by the building society for example and insufficient funds were raised at sale to cover the full debt then the debt remaining would be incorporated within the bankruptcy order and unenforceable after discharge.

10
Default Notices

What are they?
A default notice is a form which must be issued by the creditor for all debts regulated by the Consumer Credit Act before any court action is commenced, if the creditor is demanding the full payment of the monies owed before the due date.

It is therefore not required if the creditor is only claiming the arrears. For example, goods taken over a twenty-week period at £5.00 per week repayment schedule. If the twenty week period has expired then no default notice need be issued prior to any court action (i.e. the issuing of a county court summons) or alternatively if the creditor is commencing court action for the arrears only, within the twenty week period.

However if for example there has been a default in the payment schedule and by the tenth week the creditor wishes to sue for the full amount owing (20 * 5.00% =£100.00) then due to the fact that the creditor is requiring earlier payment than agreed of the full amount a default notice must be served upon the consumer/debtor.

The actual default notice itself is not a very formal looking document but is an important one and should not be overlooked, as failure to issue a default notice if it is required is a valid defence to the court action. However if a defence is based solely upon this ground this would mean that the creditor, should they so choose, upon losing the action would invariably simply issue a default notice then pursue court action a second time round.

The default notice must contain a clear statement that it is a 'default notice and served under section 87 of the Consumer Credit Act 1974' along with the following information;

* what term of the agreement has been broken.
* what action is necessary by the consumer/debtor (e.g. pay the monies owing).
* what action the creditor intends to take if the consumer/debtor is unable to comply with the term/s stated.

Upon receipt of the default notice the individual is to be given at least 7 days to carry out the required action (i.e. usually pay the sum stated in the default notice).

Once the creditor has issued the default notice and the 7 day time lapse has expired the creditor is then entitled to;

* terminate the agreement
* recover any goods/land which form part of the agreement
* demand earlier payment of the money due under the agreement

Note- Simply because a default notice has been issued does not, necessarily, mean that the creditor is going to pursue a court action against the consumer/debtor and negotiations regarding a renewed repayment schedule is sometimes still possible. However if no agreement can be reached between the parties court action will invariably be brought by the creditor.

11
Credit cards

What Are They?

They are issued by banks and building societies, e.g. Mastercard, Visa etc.

Customers may have to pay an annual usage fee.

All agreements are covered by the Consumer credit act 1974. (If signed agreement)

A credit limit will be given.

Monthly statement is provided.

Repayment is down to the customer with a set minimum but no maximum payment per month.

Unpaid sums will attract interest.

Credit card debts are non-priority debts.

Repayment negotiation would be based upon 'available income' after priority expenditure.

The card user may require the card to be cut in two returned.

It is possible to retain the card, but not use it, until the debt is cleared.

Due to the fact that they fall under the Consumer Credit Act 1974, any court proceedings will be started in the County Court, by issuing County Court Summons.

As long as the debtor replies to the summons, in admission, and an offer made, the court should make an installment order if requested.

Charge Cards
(E.G. American Express and Diners)

What Are They?

In many ways very similar to 'credit cards' which permits the holder to 'pay for goods/services or obtaining cash' but with the difference that upon the receipt of the bill the "whole" amount due is to be paid.

There is no facility for a minimum payment.

Fees will be added to the bill for the late payment.

The customer will, at the onset of taking on the card, have to sign and agree to the late payment, penalty or fee structure.

The Consumer Credit Act 1974 does not apply to these cards.

Payment Default.

Court action does not have to start in the County Court and High Court writs may be issued.

If started in the High Court the debtor can request the action to be transferred to the County Court.

Installment orders can be applied for through the high court via application .If nothing is done, enforcement action (i.e. Bailiffs) will commence, usually, immediately.

Store Cards
What are they?

These cards are issued directly by retail outlets for use within a particular store.

Goods can be purchased with three different options of payment.

A) Monthly Account: The full balance is to be repaid each month. (The Consumer Credit Act 1974 does not apply).

B) Budget account: A credit limit is in place and payment is by an agreed fixed sum per month regardless of any purchases made. If the account goes into credit, some stores may pay interest. (The Consumer Credit Act 1974 applies).

C) Option account: Similar to 'credit cards'. The customer has a credit limit along with a 'minimum' monthly repayment. Interest is applied upon any unpaid sums. (The Consumer Credit Act 1974 applies).

12
Liability for debt generally

It is very common for the individual to be informed that a debt is owed by them and simply accept the fact that they are liable for discharging it.

When presented with a debt one of the first things that the individual should do is check whether they actually owe the debt in question and if the debt is enforceable.

The points to look out for are;
A) is the contract or agreement valid and / or enforceable?
B) is anyone else responsible for the debt, or jointly responsible for it?
C) can the debt be reduced?

A debt will only exist if :
A.) A valid contract or agreement has been entered into (note- contracts can be both verbal and written)
B.) A sum must be paid under legislation (i.e.-council tax Income tax etc.).
C.) There is a court order in place (i.e.- fines, county court judgement.).

The following gives specific examples regarding certain types of indebtedness.

Fuel
The supply of fuel is usually based upon either a request for the supply via documentation or verbally requested. If an individual has requested

the supply of fuel and / or one person has always paid for the supply of fuel then it is that person who is deemed to be liable for the bill

A fuel company may try an argue that someone other than the person named upon the bill is also liable. This is referred to as the ' beneficial users ' argument .

In other words although your name is not on the bill you have had use of the fuel (i.e. gas , electric) therefore you are liable. This should be challenged. There is no legal point on which the fuel supplier can extract payment from other occupants whether that be a partner or otherwise, however it has been known for the courts to rule in the favour of the 'beneficial user' argument in certain cases.

If the individual who had requested the fuel supply or has always paid it leaves the property or refuses to pay for whatever reason, any other person in the property wishing to use the fuel supply should contact the supplier and ask to take over the usage and billing. This will indicate that the previous supply was in someone else's name.

Death
Many relatives feel that they become liable for the debt of a person who has died , especially spouses . Generally an individual is not personally liable for these debts of another, regardless of the relationship, unless that is they are "jointly and severally " liable. The debt of a deceased is paid out of the estate and if the estate has insufficient funds the debt dies with them.
There are certain exceptions to the above rule, which are;

Tenancies.
If the tenancy passes from the deceased by succession, the assignment may involve taking over any rent arrears if they cannot be paid out of the deceased's estate. It is possible for the landlord to bring possession proceedings related to the arrears against a succeeding tenant.

Mortgages.

This debt would remain outstanding on the property even if it passed to a new owner via inheritance, unless covered by insurance on death.

Council tax.

Due to the fact that council tax falls under the 'joint and several' liability rule any arrears at the date of death become the responsibility of the surviving partner.

Utility/Services. (I.e.-gas, electricity, water, telephone etc.)

If the billing for the existing services were in the deceased's name, the general rule is 'paid out of the estate or the debt dies with the deceased'.

It is important that the surviving partner contacts the suppliers informing them of the death and requests new accounts to be opened in the name of the surviving individual. It may arise upon contacting the supplier that they intimate responsibility for the deceased persons account lies with the surviving partner, no agreement for the responsibility should be given as the individual is not responsible for the debt/s.

Joint and Several Liability

This means that each person is responsible for the whole of the debt. If one party doesn't pay then the creditor is entitled to pursue the other person for the full amount owed. This will only occur where agreements are entered into 'jointly or legislation dictates so (i.e.- council tax, water charges, rent arrears, mortgage arrears of jointly occupied properties and usually business partnerships).

Minors (under 18)

A minor cannot make a " legally " enforceable contract and therefore creditors can not take court action to recover the debt. The only exception to the rule is if the contract was for "necessities" such as for example " food, clothes, medicine and drink ".

Guarantors

Certain credit agreements such as for example bank loans, hire purchase or mortgages may require "guarantors " or " sureties" to be party to the agreement. If an individual stands as a guarantor she/he is bound by the terms of the agreement. In other words if the individual (first party) fails to pay the guarantor/surety will be held liable and pursued for the debt. Undue influence should be checked for.

Undue Influence

This could occur when an agreement has been signed without, for example the bank bringing to the attention of the individual the implications connected with signing the agreement. One of the best and probably well known examples of this occurred in the case of Barclays bank v O'Brien.

A wife was told by her husband simply to sign an agreement which was to raise capital for his business. The wife signed but the agreement was deemed not to be binding upon her because of 'undue influence'. The wife should have been informed of the implications of signing and advised to take independent advice before signing the agreement. Although this was a situation surrounding the relationship of husband and wife, undue influence could occur with other close relationships.

Signature forgery

Any person whose name has been forged upon an agreement will not be liable for any debt resulting from it.

Incapacity

This would apply if the individual when entering into the agreement was unaware of what she/he was entering into. The 'not knowing' element could be caused by / or through suffering from, a mental illness or disability, learning disability or the effects of alcohol / drugs.

Insurance

Difficulty meeting payments upon a loan for example may arise through sickness. The majority of agreements taken out have an additional option of an insurance policy to cover such eventualities.

LIABILITY FOR DEBT GENERALLY

The terms of any insurance policy should be checked to see if the debt is covered during any such periods.

Are the goods or services faulty?
Debts can be challenged upon the basis that the goods / services provided were/are faulty. To negate liability on these grounds the goods/services should be rejected as soon as possible after purchase. Problems such as these should be referred to trading standards.

Consumer credit agreements in general
The majority of credit agreements fall under the Consumer Credit Act 1974. These agreements must conform to the form and content as set down under the act.

The most common things to check for in deciding liability for the debt are;
A) has the agreement been signed by the consumer and creditor?
B) are the credit terms correct?
C) have cancellation / termination notices been included, or copy's sent within the specified time limits?
D) where the agreement was entered into.

13
Magistrates Fines

Once an individual has been fined in the Magistrates court, The fine can be paid in two ways:

A) in full, or
B) by weekly installments.

If you do not pay as ordered.
The court may send out a notice informing the individual to rectify the default within a set period. However it appears that there is no requirement to send out any notice prior to the court using enforcement action to recover the debt.

If it is that the individual cannot meet the payment/s as ordered it is possible to obtain forms from the court relating to:
A) Change of Circumstances. This will ask whether the individual provided details of their financial situation at the time of the original hearing and how the individuals circumstances have changed since that date.
B) Time to Pay Outstanding Fines. This asks for the individuals personal details along with a list of incoming and outgoing finances. At the end of the form there is a place to offer a weekly/fortnightly or monthly payment. There is equally a place to request that direct deductions from state benefit be made if the individual is in receipt of income support or Job Seekers Allowance (maximum deduction is presently £2.50 per week).

It is advised that the individual facing difficulty meeting the ordered payments complete the above forms. If the above is not done and default in payment occurs enforcement action by the court will be pursued.

Enforcement which is used.
There is a great deal of discretion as how the magistrates court can enforce non-payment. Normally a distress warrant will be issued without the individuals knowledge.

The Distress Warrant / Bailiffs About.
Dealing with magistrate court bailiffs is difficult. The best option is trying to get the warrant out of the hands of the bailiffs by contacting the magistrate court (fines section) and giving details of why the fine is in default. It should be requested that the warrant be withdrawn from the bailiffs based upon a change in the individuals circumstances since the date of the fine being imposed. This is usually the best reason to use however it is unlikely that the warrant will be withdrawn in the vast majority of cases.

If it is not withdrawn.
At some point the bailiffs will attend the individuals premises. simply do not let the bailiff in and if possible remove any vehicles, nicely, parked on the driveway. If you are out when the bailiff calls do not worry the Bailiffs cannot " break in ". Equally, especially if it is summer, do not leave your windows open as they can climb through!

If no distress warrant was been issued, or successfully executed a summons will be issued with a date and time to attend the court for a means enquiry.

The Means Enquiry.
The magistrates will normally be interested in the following points:
A.) Is the defendant a fine defaulter?
B.) Does the defendant admit to the fine?
C.) Why has the defendant defaulted on payment?

D.) What is the financial situation?

Some times the defendant if unprepared may be asked to complete a " means enquiry form " immediately prior to the hearing. The form holds little information, but without previous assistance, it is a useful tool and worth completing, accurately.

The emphasis upon a 'change in circumstances and the present financial position (C and D above) is very often the basis for the magistrates decision to reduce the payment rate and / or remit part as all of the fine (write off some of the fine).

A change of circumstances can include for example:

A) Relationship breakdown.
B) Loss of job, over time.
C) Bereavement.
D) New baby.
E) Unexpected expenditure.
F) Benefit payment problems.
G) Non payment of maintenance from ex-partner.

At The End of the Means Enquiry the Magistrates have the option of;
A) Granting further time to pay the fine. This may be at the same rate of payment or a reduced rate.
B) Make an order that payments be made direct from benefits, if the individual is in receipt of income support or job seekers allowance.
C) Make an attachment of earnings order, if the individual is employed.
D) Remit the fine in part or in whole.
E) Find willful refusal and culpable neglect, which if found could lead to imprisonment.

14
Credit reference agencies

What are they, what information do they hold and how do they affect me?

There are four main credit reference agencies within the UK. The service they provide is there to facilitate those companies which provide financial services to individuals wishing to obtain a credit facility, thus permitting a quick decision by the financial establishment in respect of a request for credit from a potential customer.

In very specific terms the creditor can check whether or not the individual/s requesting the credit are a viable risk.

The information held upon an individuals file is purely factual and taken from the financial lenders themselves along with public records such as the Register of County Court Judgements.

The information provided by a lender could, for example, be the credit agreement taken out, the payment record of the individual, good or bad.

The information from the public registers is taken from the electoral role which enables names and addresses to be checked, the register of county court judgements which also include records of administration orders and the bankruptcy and individual voluntary arrangement register along with information relating to property repossessions.

The information held upon the files of a credit reference agency is held for a period of six years and then deleted.

When an individual requests a credit facility the creditor will check the name and address against the file held by the credit reference agency before giving a decision. The fact that a credit facility is declined does

not in its entirety mean there is an adverse credit scoring. It could for example be due to a policy decision made by the creditor.

When a credit check is made it is only made against the individual requesting the credit facility and not any family members or the like. It is often thought that credit reference agencies hold what is commonly called a 'blacklist' or use a 'red circling' system that depicts bad credit risks on areas, addresses or groups. This is not the case. Only information from the above mentioned sources (lenders/public registers) is held on file and no opinions are held or given regarding any individuals credit history.

It is very simply a 'library' of factual information relating to an individuals credit history and good or bad payment records during the life of the credit facility being provided.

It is the individuals right under section 159 of the Consumer Credit Act 1974 to obtain any information held upon a credit reference agency file against the individuals name. This request can be made at any time but it is usually the refusal of credit, which often triggers any request from the individual.

In these circumstances the individual should contact the creditor within twenty-eight days of refusal and make a request, in writing, for the name and address of the credit reference agency used in respect of the credit application. The creditor is obliged to provide this information, in writing, within seven days.

It is up to the individual to contact the respective credit reference agency directly to see their file, which is to be made in writing with a fee of £2, payable with the request.

Upon receiving the information held on file any errors can be corrected by following the enclosed additional information accompanying the actual file.

15
Council Tax

As we are all aware council tax is a local taxation charged and initially collected by the local authority. What therefore happens if it is not paid and it results in a debt to the local authority?

The first stage will be the receipt of reminder letters requesting the individual make the payment stated. If no payment of the required sum is made or no arrangement entered into to via a repayment schedule to clear the arrears the local authority will issue a summons via the magistrates court to obtain a liability order to recover the debt.

The liability order will automatically be granted by the Magistrates court as there is no need for the court, at this time, to consider any facts related to the debt stated. If there is a dispute over the amount claimed by the local authority this should be taken up with the local authority-rating department and/or through a valuation tribunal. The only defence to put before the court stopping the issue of the liability order is that the debt claimed has been paid in full.

For the purposes of the following text it will be assumed that the sum claimed is due and the liability order granted.

Once the liability order has been obtained by the local authority they can use a choice of methods at their disposal to try and enforce payment of the debt. At this stage, even though the liability order has been obtained negotiations regarding a repayment schedule will still be possible.

However if no repayment schedule is arranged then the following methods of enforcement can be utilised to recover the debt in question:

A) If the individual is on income support or job seekers allowance a request, by the local authority, can be made to the benefits agency to make direct deductions from the benefit at a set rate per week.

B) If the individual is employed an attachment of earnings order can be applied for through the county court. If granted this would mean that the individuals employer would be informed to deduct a set amount from the weekly or monthly pay of the individual prior to paying the employee. The amount deducted is then paid to the local authority by the employer.

C) There is an option of the local authority to bring bankruptcy proceedings against the individual if the debt exceeds £750.

D) The local authority may attempt to obtain a charging order, via the county court, on the individuals property to which the debt relates to. This, in simple terms, means that when the property is sold the debt will be repaid out of the proceeds of the sale. A charging order will only be an option if the arrears exceed £1000.

It is rare that the local authority would pursue C or D above as apart from A or B above the favoured method of enforcement by the local authority is to instruct bailiffs to recovery the debt.

If the bailiffs are used the following series of events will ensue:

A local authority can withdraw bailiffs at any time, however it is often difficult to persuade them to do so. If the Bailiff is instructed, they will attempt to levy (which simply means entering the individuals property taking control of the goods) on goods of the individual. A 'warning letter' must be sent to the individual at least fourteen days prior to the first visit by the bailiff to levy distress. The information contained in the 'warning letter' will state;

A) That a liability order has been granted against the debtor and the amount for which the liability order has been made.

B) Unless the amount stated is paid within a fourteen-day period the case may be handed over to the bailiff's, which would incur further costs to the individual in relation to the fees charged by the bailiff. A copy of the schedule of fees must accompany the letter.

C) The address and telephone number of the local authority for communication purposes.

It should be noted that there is no notification in the letter in relationship to contacting the local authority at this stage to negotiate a repayment schedule via installments. This has been standard practice and should be continued.

The individual may pay, or offer to pay, the whole amount of the debt and outstanding charges. If this is done the local authority must accept the payment or offer and instruct the Bailiff not to proceed. However the local authority is not obliged to accept repayments by installments but most do in practice. If the local authority accepts a repayment programme and this breaks down, it is at the discretion of the local authority whether they re-instruct the Bailiff. A new liability order is not required, but must notify the Bailiff of the new/current amount outstanding.

If the debt is paid prior to a levy being obtained no goods may be levied upon. If payment is made after seizure, this must be accepted by the billing authority and the individuals goods must not be sold.

The Bailiff will try to levy on the individuals goods to enforce the debt, anywhere within England and Wales, and can attempt to do so at anytime.

There is no legal right for the bailiff to enter the individuals home. However once peaceable entry has been obtained the bailiff can use force on any further visit.

If the bailiff cannot get access to the individuals premises they may try to argue the they have constructively seized goods that can be seen. A High Court decision held that in order to levy goods the bailiff must gain entry. Therefore without entry to the premises there can be no Levy. If the bailiff cannot gain entry they may try again. There is no set amount of times that an attempted levy can occur. If no goods have been levied it is not illegal to hide or remove goods in case of another visit by the bailiff.

The bailiff may attempt to levy on goods not in the debtors premises, by taking goods from other places, if peaceable entry is effected. i.e. from garden sheds/garages, place of work or a vehicle parked in the road.

The goods that are levied must belong to the individual. It should be noted that the individual does not have to answer any questions the bailiff may put to them. However, it is sometimes in the individuals best interest to communicate with the bailiff especially if a peaceable entry has been gained.

If entry is gained the bailiff will levy on enough goods to cover the debt. This is usually a surprise to the debtor. This is due to the small amount that the goods will eventually be sold for, which is usually a fraction of the real value.

When the bailiff has levied distress. The bailiff doing so will be required to;
A) Leave a further copy of the original warning letter
B) The name of the bailiff who made the levy inserted upon the warning letter
C) A revised memorandum of the amount owed by the debtor
D A copy of any walking (or close) possession agreement entered into.

Generally the bailiff will levy on any personal item, some exceptions are insurance policies, clothing in use (i.e. being worn or carried). If the bailiff attempted to remove a ring or watch by force this would be tantamount to assault.

Certain goods cannot be levied such as;

A) Clothes, bedding, furniture, household equipment and items needed to meet the basic domestic needs of the debtor and family, along with any tools, books, vehicles and other items necessary for work.
B) Goods that are not the property of the person named on the liability order cannot be seized, nor can goods that have already been levied for another debt (i.e. rent for example).
C) Goods which are under a Hire Purchase or conditional sale agreement. However goods on a credit sale agreement can be levied, as the debtor owns these even though full payment may not yet be complete.
D) Rented goods are also exempt from distress, such as a Television for example. As are leased goods.
E) Goods which belong to the individual if the person is a bankrupt.

The bailiff is permitted to levy on goods which are jointly owned by the individual and another person. In the situation of the individual and spouse/ partner the bailiff will invariably argue that the goods are jointly owned. However if the goods are solely owned by the spouse/ partner the bailiff should be informed and the goods not levied.

The bailiff has no power to levy goods which do not belong to the individual named on the liability order. The bailiff should tread with caution and ensure that the goods seized do in fact belong to the debtor. The true owner may wish to prove ownership. This could be done by showing receipts of purchase (credit cards, cheque stubs or alternatively making a statutory declaration of ownership).

After the Levy has occurred the goods will be impounded (this simply means the individual looses control of the goods and control is placed in the hands of the bailiff). This may take various forms, however the most common form is the bailiff will require the debtor to enter into a walking possession agreement.

Once a valid walking possession agreement has been signed it is illegal for the individual to dispose of, or remove the goods impounded from the premises. It also means that the bailiff has the power to return later and use force, if required, to gain entry to the premises.

If the walking possession agreement is made the goods will not usually be removed from the premises unless negotiations about repayment have broken down or failed. The individual retains use of the goods as long as it will not cause damage to them.

The individual will be charged a fee for each day the walking possession agreement continues, this will be added to the outstanding debt owed. It is therefore prudent to pay the debt as soon as possible, to avoid escalating charges.

It is imperative that if peaceable entry has not been gained then no walking possession agreement should be signed and if entry has initially been gained by the bailiff only the person named on the liability order should sign any walking possession agreement and this must be at the time of the levy. A copy of the walking possession agreement must then be given to the individual.

If the recovery procedure culminates with a sale of the individuals goods this will generally take place five days after the Levy. Sale of the individuals goods is not permitted if the individual pays or tenders the sums due prior to sale. Upon sale the bailiff's costs are recovered first out of the sale proceeds. Sale will be by public auction.

The bailiff may give up, if this occurs then they will inform the local authority that no levy was possible. They may include other relevant information. i.e. their professional opinion as to any availability of goods that may be worth levying. At this point the local authority may choose to go back to the Magistrates court for a Committal Hearing / Means Enquiry.

The Committal Hearing / Means Enquiry.
If the local authority chooses to commit the individual to prison for non-payment of the debt a court hearing will be fixed at the Magistrates court. At the hearing the court will decide whether the individual has shown 'willful refusal' or 'culpable neglect' in respect of paying the debt.

What do the two terms mean?
Willful Refusal.
This means that there has been a deliberate and/or intentional decision taken by the individual not to pay the debt, even though it was within the individuals means to pay the debt.

Culpable Neglect.
This means that there must have been, not just, neglect on behalf of the individual to pay the debt but it must be shown that there was an element of carelessness involved in the neglect. In other words non-payment of the debt could have been avoided with due care and attention, given the individuals financial circumstances at the time the debt arose.

If the court reaches the conclusion that there is evidence to show the above two factors are correct then it is possible for the court to commit the individual to prison for a period not exceeding six months. It is however usual to find that, even if proved, the court will suspend the warrant committing the individual to prison on the order that payment of the debt be made by installments.

If the court finds neither of the two above factors present they can order that all or part of the debt be written off.

16
The Bailiff

As outlined in the previous chapter, the standard advice is do not let them into your home as they have no legal right to enter your premises, if they have not gained entry on a previous visit.

The reasons behind the above statement stem from the fact that the bailiffs powers of entry to the individuals premises go from nothing to everything once they have, peaceably, obtained entry. Once entry has been obtained their powers increase dramatically in as much that if a successful Levy has been completed on the initial visit they can, if needed, force entry to remove goods that have initially been placed / taken under their legal control.

If the bailiff is attending on the first visit and has previously not gained entry then as above stated simply do not let them in.

The things to bear in mind if you know or are aware that the creditor is using bailiffs to attempt to enforce payment of the debt are;

A) vehicles parked neatly on the driveway or on the road in front of the individual house are easy pickings and will be levied straight away without any need to obtain entry to the individuals premises.

B) Garages left open will present the same easy prey regarding the content to the calling bailiff.

C) Although the bailiff cannot force entry to your premises, they can:

· climb through open windows, using ladders if available. Open already partially open windows.
· open doors which are closed but unlocked and equally open doors which are left ajar.
· break open internal doors. This element is worthy of an additional cautionary note if the individuals premises has an attached garage with a connecting door to the main dwelling which would mean that entry via the above methods to the garage will lead to an effective entry to the main dwelling house.

The reference made above to internal doors as opposed to external ones becomes a somewhat grey area if the individual resides in a bedsit or shared house as there would presumably be one main entrance classed as an external door and the remainder within the property being internal doors.

Exceptions to the above, general, rules are;

· Sheriffs officer. These are bailiffs who are used in connection with the recovery procedure from the High court. They may force entry to any separate and non-domestic premises of the individual that are not connected to, or within the grounds of the main dwelling house.
· County court bailiff. These are bailiffs who are used in connection with the recovery procedure from the County court. They may force entry into buildings that are not connected to the main dwelling house, including those within the grounds of the house.
· Private bailiff. These are used predominately by the local authority, Child Support Agency, and Magistrates court. The private bailiff is not permitted to force entry.

If the individual has not let the bailiff into the home and is therefore unable to recover the debt the 'warrant' will be returned to the court or the creditor (for example the local authority). At this stage the following will occur:

· If the bailiff was from the County court, notification will be given to the creditor that no levy was possible and it is up to the creditor to pursue further, alternative, recovery action if they so choose.

- If the bailiff was attempting to recover the debt relating to: Council Tax, Magistrates Court Fines, Maintenance and Child Support Maintenance the refusal to permit entry by the individual will lead to a Means Enquiry/Committal Hearing before the magistrates court.

Throughout the whole of the above procedure, with the exception of warrants issued in respect of Magistrates court fines, it is possible to negotiate with the creditor regarding a repayment schedule and for the creditor to withdraw bailiff action.

If the situation culminates in a Means Enquiry/Committal Hearing the individual is strongly advised to seek professional help from organisations such as the Citizens Advice Bureau or Federation of Independent Advice Agencies which are listed in the telephone directories.

Index